T0295571

Embodying Integral Development

In this fourth and final volume of the CARE-ing for Integral Development series, Ronnie Lessem integrates all that has come before in terms of: Community activation; Awakening integral consciousness; and institutionalized Research. Here he focuses on individual and community development alongside that of the organization or society, and sets it in the context of an integral economy.

The four critical success factors identified in recognizing and releasing integral development aligned with CARE are:

- GROUNDING – linking up with and building upon existing local and global movements for socio-economic development;
- EMERGENCE – maintaining interconnected focus;
- NAVIGATING – locating and developing GENE-ius in a particular community/society;
- EFFECTING – committing to resolving an issue and identifying the most fertile development path.

Embodying Integral Development offers a comprehensive system of accreditation. Supported by examples and illustrations of CARE, this book makes a case for Integral Development as a whole. It argues that it is a qualitative means of self-assessment rather than a quantitative one, focused on engagement, immersion and interpretation, as well as evaluation, rather than empirical verification.

Ronnie Lessem is the Co-Founder of Trans4m, Geneva. He has been a management educator and consultant in Africa, Asia, Europe and America and is the author of over thirty books on the development of self, business and society.

Transformation and Innovation

Series editors: Ronnie Lessem and Alexander Schieffer

This series on enterprise transformation and social innovation comprises a range of books informing practitioners, consultants, organization developers, development agents and academics how businesses and other organizations, as well as the discipline of economics itself, can and will have to be transformed. The series prepares the ground for viable twenty-first-century enterprises and a sustainable macroeconomic system. A new kind of R & D, involving social as well as technological innovation, needs to be supported by integrated and participative action research in the social sciences. Focusing on new, emerging kinds of public, social and sustainable entrepreneurship originating from all corners of the world and from different cultures, books in this series will help those operating at the interface between enterprise and society to mediate between the two and will help schools teaching management and economics to re-engage with their founding principles.

For a full list of titles in this series, please visit www.routledge.com/business/series/TANDI

CARE-ing for Integral Development Series

Volume 1
Community Activation for Integral Development
Ronnie Lessem

Volume 2
Awakening Integral Consciousness
A Developmental Perspective
Ronnie Lessem

Volume 3
Innovation Driven Institutional Research
Towards Integral Development
Ronnie Lessem

Volume 4
Embodying Integral Development
A Holistic Approach
Ronnie Lessem

Embodying Integral Development
A Holistic Approach

Ronnie Lessem

Routledge
Taylor & Francis Group

LONDON AND NEW YORK

First published 2017
by Routledge
2 Park Square, Milton Park, Abingdon, Oxon OX14 4RN

and by Routledge
711 Third Avenue, New York, NY 10017

Routledge is an imprint of the Taylor & Francis Group, an informa business

British Library Cataloguing in Publication Data
A catalogue record for this book is available from the British Library.

Library of Congress Cataloging in Publication Data
A catalog record for this book has been requested

ISBN: 978-1-138-74052-5 (hbk)
ISBN: 978-1-315-18342-8 (ebk)

Typeset in Times New Roman
by Swales & Willis, Exeter, Devon, UK

Contents

PART III
Realization path: institutional research to
embody development   93

Figures

Tables

Prologue

Embodying integral development
Integral enterprise and economy

Introduction to CARE

In this fourth and final volume we integrally and developmentally Embody now, all that has come functionally (*CARE*) and structurally (CARE) before, within an ultimately integral enterprise and/or economy. This involves respectively Community activation-and-building Care Circles; Awakening integral consciousness-and-Actualizing an innovation eco-system; innovation driven, institutionalized Research-and-Recognizing an inter-institutional genealogy. As such we focus on individual and com-munal, organizational and societal, development, functionally, set in the context of an integral enterprise and economy, structurally (see Figure 0.1 below). Embodying *integral Rounds* of development in this way includes but transcends education, because we encompass successive and interac-tive rounds of individual and *collective* – communal, organizational and societal – development (Schieffer and Lessem, 2004).

Moreover, and as has been the case before, we shall also now be pursuing each path – relational, renewal and reasoned realization – integrally and rhythmically in turn. As such we shall be incorporating Grounding, Emergence, Navigation and Effect in each case, thereby rec-ognizing and releasing GENE-ius. Finally, then, we regard the relational path as most closely aligned with community activation/Care Circles, with a view to awakening integral consciousness/innovation ecosystem; the renewal path as aligned with awakening consciousness/innovation ecosystem with a view to institutionalized research/inter-institutional genealogy; and finally the path of reasoned realization as aligned with innovation driven institutionalized research/inter-institutional geneal-ogy with a view, ultimately, to embodying integral development/integral enterprise and economy.

We now turn, CARE wise, to the first four chapters on the relational path, in this Embodiment case following the full *integral rhythm* for each

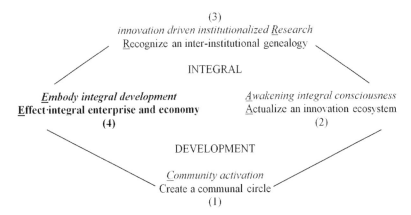

Figure 0.1 CARE and CARE

path, from grounding to emergence to navigation to effect respectively, involving, relationally, personal and communal engagement, functionally and structurally.

Relational path: personal and communal embodiment

Community activation to Awakening integral consciousness

Relational ground: Goko – individual/communal leadership, Chapter 1

The "southern" *relational* Embodiment of Integral Development begins, then, with personal and communal engagement, for us, in the African south, specifically exemplified in Zimbabwe, thereby grounding the relational path. For Ezekiah Chasamhuka Benjamin as such, as an operations manager with an African difference, it is almost impossible to "train" someone to have the spirit to succeed (Mamukwa *et al.*, 2014). *It is only through sublimation of the ego and the will to evolve, coming directly from the person, that the spirit is cultivated to perform.* To uncover this, more specifically, Benjamin turns, functionally, to what he terms *Goko leadership – passing the good on –* and the four constituents, so to speak, of its DNA. Structurally, as we shall see, Benjamin begins by creating a learning community, as a "southern" communal equivalent of "northern" study circles.

By analogy then, overall, such an African functional DNA has four local constituents: A is for adenine; G is for guanine; C is for cytosine; and T is for thymine. Benjamin starts, analogously, with *(A) Dance or Rhythm as*

Grounding; turns second to (G) Selflessness or Sacrifice (Emergence); then to (C) Knowledge and Communication (Navigation); and finally to (T) the Spirit of Success (Effect). We turn, then, from individual and communal leadership to organizational knowledge creation, still on the relational path.

Relational emergence: calabash – group knowledge sharing, Chapter 2

Second and organizationally, in an emergent "south-eastern" (Zimbabwean–Japanese), now local–global guise, for Human Resource Director Liz Mamukwa, the metaphor of a calabash is used, as a basis for knowledge sharing, embodying communal and organizational development (Mamukwa *et al.*, 2014). For the calabash was among one of the first African plants to be cultivated in the world. Although it is edible, it was cultivated not for its culinary qualities but rather for its use as a container, as a musical instrument, as a bottle or a pipe. In Africa the big calabash is used today mostly as a container for water, beer or other non-alcoholic drink such as *maheu* (an opaque drink made out of fermented maize meal). The calabash can also, and even more importantly for our purposes, be used as a musical instrument (*hosho*) to bring rhythmic harmony to bear.

Mamukwa then imagined such a rhythm forming a harmonic sound among the machines of her factory, that is, at Turnall Holdings, manufacturing asbestos roofing, in Zimbabwe. The metaphoric rhythm is further accentuated through a GENE cycle – Grounding, Emerging, Navigating, Effecting – of knowledge creation that is ongoing, day in and day out, whether there is a project happening or not. It should ideally become a way of life at the workplace if the enterprise claims to be a knowledge creating organization, within which she also established an innovation ecosystem. By extension, if this rhythm is instilled in the people at work, what is to say that they cannot spread this to their homes and villages?

Relational navigation: GENE rhythm – social innovation, Chapter 3

If third, then, as a next chapter in Embodying Integral Development now societally, we are to resolve such thorny problems as those of poverty and injustice, climate change and the ravages of closed societies, we have to rhythmically plumb the depths, in each societal-and-worldly case, that is, over and above the local relational leadership and local–global knowledge sharing conducted hitherto.

It is thereby not enough to "originate" (grounding) a new form of enterprise, say a "social" enterprise. Such a new enterprise, rather, needs a substantively new foundation (emerging), or functioning. It requires radical emancipation (navigation) from prevailing structures and processes, and there is ultimately a need for full transformation (effecting). To say then, at a macro level, that state-controlled socialism has failed, and therefore we need to retain one or other form of free enterprise based capitalism, for us, integrally speaking, just won't wash. Such an approach will never reach the great unwashed! There is no emancipation. No transformation. Just adaptation. *What we are therefore in need of is social innovation* (Lessem and Schieffer, 2010b)*, thereby following our integral GENE rhythm and realms, in the latter case nature, culture, technology and economy, as all-round polity, ultimately contained within an institutional genealogy.*

Relational effect: integral realms – societal transformation, Chapter 4

The so-called "realms" behind our "four world" thereby integral approach – natural, cultural, technological and economic – build on an integral perspective of economy-and-society as well as of enterprise (Lessem and Schieffer, 2009). As such we reject the conventionally twofold divisions between capitalism and socialism, north and south, or east and west, as being static and divisive, rather than dynamic and inclusive, worldly wise. Indeed, the original development of human communities and societies followed a fourfold rhythm. Tens of thousands of years ago, when the first human communities were forged, they formed a deep and immediate relational connection with nature as well as locality. It was only much later, that cultural artefacts were added to such communities. From there communities started to organize themselves more systematically, and developed initial simple structures, roles and positions. It took a long time, until such communities started engaging in trade with other communities. In other words, *the relational connection came first, later to be followed by cultural renewal and socio-economic realization, thereby partaking in overall societal transformation.*

These initial differentiations mirror, to this day, the core life-giving "realities" of human worldly communities and societies: a "southern" enterprise function of *community building* focused societally on nature and community through environmentalism; an "eastern" such function of *conscious evolution* focusing on culture and spirituality through what might be termed culturalism; a northern enterprise function of *knowledge creation* focusing on systematic knowledge (science), technology and governance structures, in the context of social democracy; and a western function of *sustainable development* focusing on economics (including trade) and finance, and creating economic opportunity.

In the next four chapters, following now the path of "south-eastern" renewal, from grounding to effect, we ground ourselves, first societally, in the integral state. The path of renewal than embodies communal and societal, self, and organizational, development.

Renewal path: self, organizational and societal embodiment

Awakening integral consciousness to institutional research

Grounding renewal: towards the integral state, Chapter 5

The state, for Somali American political scientist Ahmed Samatar, founding Dean of Macalester College's Institute for Global Citizenship, is not some formless thing. Rather he suggests, heuristically, four main elements that make up the state. Their commonwealth as per our Community activation, in our CARE terms, provides the underlying *grounding*; a state regime promotes *emergence*; a competent administration underlies *navigation*; and able leadership embodies a potentially, ultimately integral *effect* (Samatar and Samatar, 2002).

More specifically, such a formative commonwealth, first then, incorporates intimate association and a full spirit of public belonging. A reformative political regime, thereafter, secures acceptance and legitimacy in wider society. Third, a competent newly normative administration provides reliable, trustworthy public institutions. Moreover, for the Samatars, able, *transformative leadership gives rise to an ultimately integral state, surpassing the prior developmental, and transcending the "cadaverous" and "prebendal" (self protective) states that came before.*

Emergent renewal: enterprise to institutional integration, Chapter 6

We now turn from societal to enterprise renewal. In the process of our renewing management and organization, we maintain that, in pursuit of a prospectively "integral" rhythm, *personal enterprise* origination (Grounding), by one individual or another, in one place/society or another, is followed by the establishment of a *managerial and organizational* foundation (Emergence). Thereafter, *individual leadership* has its subsequently emancipatory place (Navigation), only when set, systemically, within a developing self, and organization, as well as an explicitly recognized, evolving *society*. Finally and ultimately for us, *integral* transformation (Effect) follows when all of this is not only differentiated but also integrated: self and community, organization and society, in a particular world, in relation to other worlds, psychologically and culturally. Thereby, altogether, we recognize and release a particular GENE-ius (Lessem, 2016).

In this way we have given rise to the new notion of an "Integrator" in the twenty-first century. Such an integrator emerges as a further evolution, of personal entrepreneurship (or "intrapreneurship") in the nineteenth century, management in the twentieth, and leadership in the twenty-first, embodying all of this, as we shall see, in integral organizational development, set within an innovation ecosystem, comprising such stewardship, alongside catalyzation, research and facilitation. What, then, about the navigation of integral development, or the renewal of economy and society, as a whole?

Navigate renewal: releasing economic GENE-ius, Chapter 7

The four "critical success factors" that we have identified in recognizing and releasing the economic genius, specifically, of a particular society, aligned with CARE, as well as our integral rhythm, are as follows:

1 *grounding – community activation*: linked up with, and built upon, existing local and global movements for socio-economic development;
2 *emergence – awakening integral consciousness*: maintain interconnected focus, middle–up–down–across;
3 *navigating – innovation driven institutionalized research* for locating and developing economic gene-ius in a particular community/society; as well as ultimately
4 *effecting – Embodying Integral Development*: commit to resolving a real burning issue and identify the most fertile development path (Lessem and Schieffer, 2010a).

More specifically and first, for prominent American social and environmental activist Paul Hawken (2008), the large-scale movements to which he alludes today have three basic roots: *environmental activism, social justice initiatives, and indigenous cultures' resistance to globalization, all of which have become intertwined.* A top-down approach, second, would start with the overarching *macro*-economic system, as per, for example, capitalism or socialism, both of which, for us, lack both academic–theoretical and practical–contextual integrity. On the other hand, "bottom-up" individual *micro* enterprises or communities in isolation, are by far too weak in themselves to become beacons of development. So for us, and our Trans4m associates, be it a Sekem in Egypt or a Sarvodaya in Sri Lanka, *the place to start is in the mesa middle, working up–down–across.*

Third, as we shall see, as far as *social research and development* is concerned, through our inter-institutional genealogy, *schools or universities (navigating) are part of an integral genealogical and newly global whole*, including local community (grounding), local–global sanctuary (emergence) and global–local laboratory (effecting). <u>Fourth</u> and finally, the *long-term commitment to a burning issue, which sustains efforts to build a new kind of "relevant" enterprise, requires a strong moral inspiration.* For Ibrahim Abouleish's Sekem Group, in Egypt for example, it is to reclaim the desert and restore the earth, drawing on "the vitality of the sun" (meaning of Sekem) (Abouleish, 2005). Such an inspiration has to be *morally authentic* to the core protagonists and to the particular context, and, at the same time, needs to be *enriched by a compelling universal truth*, in his case aligned with the overarching principles of ecology, ultimately contained within an institutional genealogy.

Effecting renewal: bridging the gulf – societal renaissance, Chapter 8

Finally, on the path of renewal with a view to embodying integral development, we turn to overall societal renaissance, and the extraordinary contemporary case of Oman – *bridging the Gulf* between Africa, Asia and the Arab world in that respect. Retracing steps, we find that thoughts about life, about relations between people, and ultimately with God, began to interest the young Omani Sultan Qaboos at an early age (Plekhanov, 2004). Among the many books he read, a collection of Shakespeare's tragedies compiled by an Arab writer impressed him most. He was already reaching out from the Omani local to the European global, albeit in this specifically English context.

Having learned to read at five, the future Sultan enjoyed immersing himself in a complex world of human passions. But the most important book that the heir to the throne discovered for himself was the Holy Qur'an. At every stage of his life it has been his spiritual fulcrum. *Grounded overall then relationally in Arab (Middle East), Swahili (East Africa) and Balochi (near East) worlds that constituted Oman, emerging renewal wise through such, blending tradition and modernity, navigating reason wise though shura-based democracy*, Oman through Sultan Qaboos over the past three decades has ultimately effected its social and economic realization through distributed oil revenues.

We now turn from the relational and renewal paths to the culminating path of reasoned realization, whereby, as we have invariably intimated, the "north-west" (Europe and America) needs to build on the "south-eastern" rest (Africa, South America and Asia). As such we focus on research, learning and development, starting out with a primary school and ending with an integral society.

Reasoned realization: research/learning/development

Innovative institutional research to embodying integral development

Educating senses at school – ground self/community realization,
Chapter 9

The kindergarten Otona Župančiča, Slovenska Bistrica in Slovenia, will soon be turning 70 (Piciga *et al.*, 2016). If this was a period in human life, it could be said that the kindergarten had already reached its mature age. However, it stays vital with the influx of new generations of children, parents and employees. Generations of children get to know each other through the kindergarten and parents are given the opportunity of networking, which the kindergarten fondly supports. Each family has something to offer to others, but all the school is also vulnerable and even the strongest family can face an obstacle. Networking often helps people overcome various situations with which they are confronted. The kindergarten works on five protective factors: *resilience of parents; supporting social networks; knowledge about parenthood and child development; actual support in times of crisis; and child's healthy social and emotional development.*

That sense of social responsibility also led Slovenska Bistrica to the project originated by the Institute for Ethics and Values of the Slovenian Academy of Sciences and Arts. After receiving an invitation for cooperation from the institute, the kindergarten reviewed its program on Ethics and Values in Education and recognized the principles, values and actions that were considered important and according to which the kindergarten works. "*The institute's intention was to expand and deepen awareness on the role of ethics, values and bioethics in forming a common future in all important areas of social activities, especially in education*".

In fact the kindergarten in Slovenia and the MedLabs Group of medical laboratories in Jordan, though geographically and vocationally far apart, have more in common than might immediately meet the eye.

Enterprise learning/development: emerging group realization,
Chapter 10

The unfolding story of MedLabs, an extraordinary group of medical laboratories, based primarily in Jordan, but also operating in the Sudan, in Irbil in Kurdistan, in Palestine and in Kuwait, in the context of *revitalizing its moral core*, is told here by co-founder Manar Al Nimer, who is also engaged in our Trans4m PhD program. Manar then takes the story of herself and of MedLabs on, individually, organizationally and societally, in her own words: *beyond a one man show*.

> Every moment from our birth till we die we are exposed to new challenges. *At every moment we learn new things, we see new people, we talk to new people, we are exposed to new cultures and beliefs, we face problems, we suffer from diseases, we graduate, we get married, we give birth, we lose loved ones and we have to deal with all of these experiences one way or another.* These are the challenges we face during our life journey. Jordan meanwhile, that small country which has been my home throughout my adult life, with its limited resources, no oil and scarcity of water has the ambition, determination and will to stand side by side with the developed nations, albeit in its own authentic way.
>
> It has one of the highest percentages of qualified manpower who enjoy pioneering and innovative capabilities. Time has shown that the strength of Jordan is in its people and their ability to overcome one regional crisis after the other, through organizational and societal learning, and produce several successful organizations on the world stage, like Medlabs Group, despite the difficulties it faces locally and regionally.

We now turn from school and enterprise to our inter-institutional genealogy.

Institutional genealogy: effect integral development in Africa, Chapter 11

For American cultural historians McNeely and Wolverton (2008) penultimately, to whom we were first introduced in our previous volume, *Innovation Driven Institutionalized Research*, today's epochal historical events, most recently climate change and economic crises, have determined that *the laboratory, not the university, will continue to exercise a strong influence on learning and knowledge creation, especially in the natural sciences.* Above all, the ascendancy of the laboratory is reshaping the basic missions of other institutions, like indeed universities, pushing some towards obsolescence while giving others a new lease of life.

We have begged to differ (Lessem *et al.*, 2013). For us, then, always firmly with our feet on the local ground, though we may reach for the global skies, our starting point is invariably a local *community* as "southern" grounding. Our next port of call, with our focus primarily in the "global south", where religion/spirituality is such an all-pervasive local–global phenomenon, after community, comes *sanctuary*, as, for us, "south-eastern" emergence. It is only thereafter that a school or *academy*, as "northern" navigation and indeed finally *laboratory* as "western" effect, comes into integral play. Indeed, our Dr Anselm Adodo, founder of Paxherbals and Pax Africana in Nigeria, as we saw in the previous volume, takes that story on from here, in his book *Community Enterprise in Africa: Communitalism as an Alternative to Capitalism* (2017). We now turn finally back to Europe.

Integral society: effect integral development in Europe, Chapter 12

Slovenia, a small country located at the heart of Europe, is finally introduced as a pilot case of an integral society and economy. *Grounded in the smell of forest, a babbling brook and soft wood, we feel Slovenia as an emergent foundation, a strong bio-energetic field capable of supporting development and thereby in tune with the essence of life; thus emancipatory navigation of Integral Green Slovenia is undertaken institutionally, with research and innovation ecologically, culturally, technologically and economically following, ultimately effecting self-sufficiency, a developmental economy, a social and a living economy.*

What has not yet been achieved, though, is to lodge this Citizens' Initiative, explicitly, as an institutionalized research project and process within one academic or research institute, in particular; instead, for the time being it is spread across a wide range of such political, economic, ecological and cultural, and institutionalized research, entities. To look at what has been achieved another way, though, while many a *community* is involved in the Citizen's Initiative (see our previous volume on *Community activation*, Chapter 8) and artist extraordinaire Marko Pogacnik is a kind of "one man cultural *sanctuary*", not to mention also the public, private and civic *laboratories* involved, as such enterprises, the closest we have to a research *academy* engaged with the initiative is Biotechnika Naklo, though the remarkable Slovenian kindergarten (see Chapter 9) Otona Župančiča Slovenska Bistrica has an active research group that has established a social innovation centre of its own.

We now turn to Chapter 1, for our grounding on the "southern" relational path for embodying now personal and communal development.

References

Abouleish, I. (2005) *Sekem: A Sustainable Community in the Egyptian Desert.* Edinburgh: Floris Books.

Adodo, A. (2017) *Community Enterprise in Africa: Communitalism as an Alternative to Capitalism.* Abingdon: Routledge.

Hawken, P. (2008) *Blessed Unrest: How the Largest Movement in the World Came into Being.* New York: Viking.

Lessem, R. (2016) *The Integrators: Beyond Leadership, Knowledge and Value Creation*. Abingdon: Routledge.

Lessem, R. and Schieffer, A. (2009) *Transformation Management: Toward the Integral Enterprise*. Abingdon: Routledge.

Lessem, R. and Schieffer, A. (2010a) *Integral Economics: Releasing the Genius of your Society*. Abingdon: Routledge.

Lessem, R. and Schieffer, A. (2010b) *Integral Research and Innovation: Transforming Enterprise and Society*. Abingdon: Routledge.

Lessem, R., Schieffer, A., Rima, S. and Tong, J. (2013) *Integral Dynamics: Cultural Dynamics, Political Economy and the Future of the University*. Abingdon: Routledge.

Mamukwa, E., Lessem, R. and Schieffer, A. (2014) *Integral Green Zimbabwe: An African Phoenix Rising*. Abingdon: Routledge.

McNeely, I. and Wolverton, L. (2008) *Reinventing Knowledge: Alexandria to the Internet*. New York: Norton.

Piciga, D., Schieffer, A. and Lessem, R. (2016) *Integral Green Slovenia: Towards a Social and Knowledge Based Society and Economy in the Heart of Europe*. Abingdon: Routledge.

Plekhanov, S. (2004) *A Reformer on the Throne: Sultan Qaboos bin Said Al Said*. Cronulla, New South Wales, Australia: Trident Press.

Samatar, A. and Samatar, A., eds (2002) *The African State*. New York: Heinemann Educational Books.

Schieffer, A. and Lessem, R. (2014) *Integral Development: Realizing the Transformative Potential of Individuals, Organizations and Societies*. Abingdon: Routledge.

Part I

Relational path

Community activation to awaken
consciousness

1 Grounding

Goko – personal and community engagement

Summary of chapter:

1 bringing in harmony and value is the grounding "dancing" element;
2 the Goko leader emerges as a good person as he/she sacrifices for our benefit;
3 navigating "*kuzivisana*" means to enable each other to know – without the other person informing another, there is no knowledge existing;
4 by way of effect with the constant spirit of accomplishment, there is greater probability of success than undertaking a task with the spirit of failure.

Goko Routungamiri: relational grounding of embodied leadership

Developmental "good" passed on through generations

This final volume, *Embodying Integral Development*, involves us in *CARE*-ing functionally for development self and community, organization and society, and CARE-ing structurally for an integral enterprise-and-society. It thereby follows from *Community activation*/Creating Care Circles, *Awakening of integral consciousness*/Actualizing an innovation ecosystem, as well as *innovation driven, institutionalized Research*/Recognizing an inter-institutional genealogy. Such complementary *CARE*/CARE then serves as a culmination, and indeed functional and structural embodiment, of what has come before. We start, as has invariably been the case for us, in grounding ourselves through the "southern" *relational* path, with the help, to begin with individually and communally, of an African visionary leader, Ezekiah Chasamhuka Benjamin (Mamukwa *et al.*, 2014). Via his *goko routungamiri*, for him as we shall see, *the developmental "good" is passed on though generations*.

Goko Routungamiri: leaving a legacy

The creation and application of *personal and communal leadership in an African context*, for Benjamin as an operations manager with a difference as we shall see, springs from his intention *to create desirable outcomes for the common good*. Such an approach to leadership, then, sadly untypical in Africa as a whole – we would argue often because of individual/institutional as well as indigenous/exogenous "southern–northern" mismatch – involves acquiring and sharing knowledge so all have a fair share of the enjoyment or pain of the collective results. Such common good also emerges out of indigenous African culture and spirituality. Goals as such are unilaterally or collectively set, but the results are then felt by learning communities across the whole enterprise.

In fact the integral African leader works, as we shall see, in the fourfold, thereby *integral* realms of first *rhythm and dance*, second *self-sacrifice*, third *knowledge and communication, and* fourth the *spirit of success* to leave a legacy, *nhaka yamusiiranwa*. The model postulates that the state of knowing alone is not enough. What is important is to have that internal, African spirit to succeed.

It is almost impossible, then, to "train" someone to have that spirit to succeed. It is only through sublimation of the ego and the will to evolve, coming directly from the person-in-community, that the spirit is cultivated

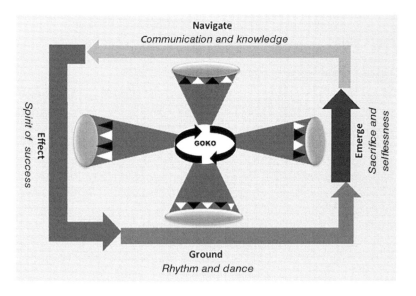

Figure 1.1 The GENE of leadership immersed in four worlds

to perform. To uncover this more specifically, Benjamin then turns to the GENE of leadership, and the four constituents, for him so to speak, of its DNA. By analogy DNA has four constituents: A is for adenine; G is for guanine; C is for cytosine; and T is for thymine. He starts, analogously, with (A) Dance or Rhythm as Grounding – our primary concern here, turns second to (G) Selflessness or Sacrifice (Emergence), then to (C) Knowledge and Communication (Navigation), and finally to (T) the Spirit of Success (Effect).

The first Goko Routungamiri gene: grounding – rhythm and dancing

The leadership GENE as a whole

The first constituent of our African leadership Gene is rhythm or danc- ing, which brings in a communal circle from the outset. Before Benjamin turns to this, though, he reviews the leadership GENE as a whole. The circular spiral depicted in Figure 1.1 above is like a tornado. The inner spirit to succeed does not function in isolation of the total human being who works with others to the benefit of all. It is in this context that a leader must be rooted in his or her culture and then interrelate with other subcultures for every sub-system in the organization to be motivated to achieve expected outcomes.

The role of rhythm and dance

Ezekiah Chasamhuka Benjamin is deeply grounded communally in African traditions. He grew up as a dancer, a young village boy who was awakened by the rhythm of his people. With time Western education took over from the sounds and rhythms of the village and what began to dominate were the rational challenges brought about by the needs of the dominantly capitalist ethos in the world as a whole. That said, and revisiting his roots, Benjamin has come up with a Musire leadership model (see Figure 1.2 below) that has African drums in circular motion at its core.

While the dictates of the world changed the behaviour of the village boy to suit the demands of nations and institutions, these world challenges and their attractions did not change the ability of the African child, according to Benjamin, to love those sounds and rhythms of his or her people. The seed sown at birth and early childhood was to blossom later on in life. In fact, to appreciate other people from different nationalities and different cultures and backgrounds, for Benjamin, one must first appreciate people from his or her small village, region and country. Leadership germinates from the

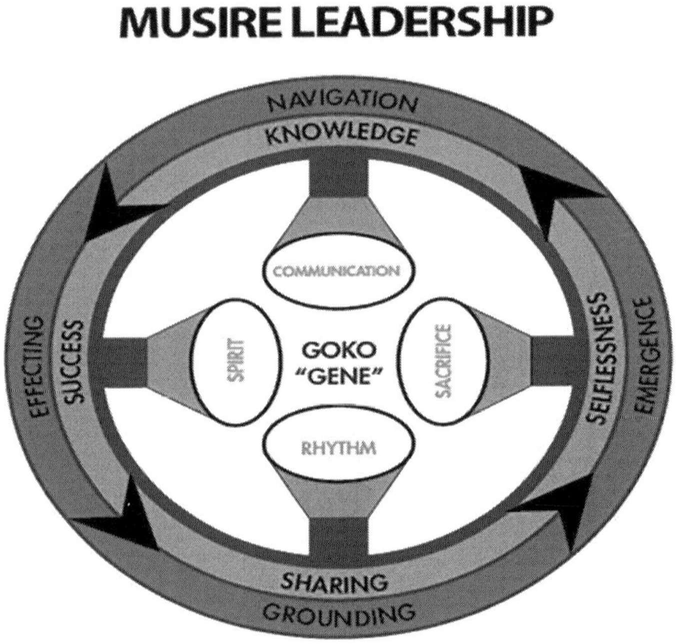

MUSIRE LEADERSHIP

Figure 1.2 Musire leadership

ecology of the people and permeates in our day-to-day behaviours to give a consistent meaning to the people at all levels in different cultural realms.

The rhythmical underpinning of the Musire leadership model

Rhythm and dancing, then, are only metaphors taken in an African context to reveal the deeper, rhythmical meaning of an emerging African leadership model. Each nation, institution and organization has got its own values, culture, systems and processes that justify its core existence. Harmony exists, for Benjamin when the culture of an institution is not in conflict with the core business of the institution. That interrelationship and the creation of expected value from interwoven systems, services and products is what Benjamin terms the *rhythm*.

The ability and the process of bringing in harmony and value is what Benjamin then terms the *grounding* "dancing" element. The precipitators of rhythm creation are the communal circle of people. The leader must understand that communal rhythm and be able to craft strategies, policies and systems that can be choreographed successfully for and by that circle, in pursuit of a common goal at a national and organizational level.

Bringing the grounded dance rhythm to Rusape Brewery

At the Rusape Brewery in rural Zimbabwe, for which Benjamin was operationally responsible – as a part of the Delta Corporation, one of Zimbabwe's largest companies –, his workers started their tasks with the beat of African drums, so that *every employee in the company heard the African drums beating; there was an internal awakening that every team member had to undergo at their own work station in order to perfect their tasks and outputs.* To those workers without any supervisory responsibilities, the sound of drums meant the resumption of the performance of tasks and duties. That act of execution of tasks after the beating of the drums was an inherent team-bonding exercise that told everyone, "We belong to the same village where we grew up listening to the same sounds and dancing to the same rhythm, so here at work we can still be united and work with one purpose."

Table 1.1 The GENE of leadership

Embodying Integral Development: Relational Grounding   *Goko Routungamiri: GENE of leadership*   Rhythm and dance to spirit of success
<ul><li>*Attributes of embodiment* – RELATIONAL PATH: Grounding – ***Goko personal and communal engagement***; Emergence – calabash of group knowledge sharing; Navigation – GENE rhythm of social innovation; Effect – integral realities/societal transformation. RENEWAL PATH: Grounding – integral state; Emergence – institutional integration; Navigation – releasing GENE-ius; Effect – societal renaissance. REASONED REALIZATION PATH: Grounding – school education for all the senses; Emergence – enterprise learning and development; Navigation – sustainable development university; Effecting – institutional genealogy.</li><li>*Integrator role*: embodied leader, e.g. ***Ezekiah Chasamhuka Benjamin***.</li><li>*GENE of leadership*: the process of ***bringing in harmony and value*** is the *grounding* "dancing" element; *emerging* through "Munhu akanaka uyu anozvipira" means he or she is a good person as ***he/ she sacrifices for our benefit***; *navigating* in a family or community involves ***"kuzivisana", meaning to enable each other to know*** – without the other person informing another, there is no knowledge existing; by way of *effect* with ***the constant spirit of accomplishment***, there is greater probability of success than undertaking a task with the spirit of failure.</li></ul>

For junior, middle and top leadership at the Brewery, the beating of the drums was a call for all these leaders to understand all their goals, systems and processes with the aim of making available resources at all levels. That act of appreciating the culture, values, objectives and systems is the real sowing of the seed of the first Gene of *Grounding* and *Relational* Leadership *embodied* in *Rhythm and Dance*. A visitor to Rusape Brewery today would think that the village has been brought to the modern organization. *The whole idea is not to bring the village to the brewery but to take the brewery to the village because organizations in Africa are manned by people from communities, whether in villages or townships.* It is those sounds and such a natural environment that motivates leaders and workers, according to Benjamin, to self-discover and to move their organizations and societies to greater heights of achievement.

The rhythm of nature: eco-enterprise and community

In their book *Transformation Management*, Lessem and Schieffer (2009) align an enterprise such as Rusape Breweries to an "Eco-Enterprise". They write,

> *Conventional wisdom has involved comparing and contrasting "transactional management" and "transformational leadership". For us this has meant merely putting old wine in new bottles, as the basic form of the enterprise remained unchanged. There is a fundamentally new form increasingly visible, which so far has been subsumed under the social enterprise: the eco-enterprise. With eco-enterprise we mean enterprises, which have a strong environmental orientation, and are deeply rooted in nature and nature's principles.*

Lessem and Schieffer go on to quote Catherine Campbell, a South African social psychologist currently based at the London School of Economics, who pointed out that, "*we have discredited our enterprising physical selves and commoditised the business living. In fact, we exist today because our foremothers foraged and gathered and, later, accomplished the transition to gardening and agriculture.*"

A Musire enterprise, for Benjamin, is different from a socially responsible enterprise, in the sense that an enterprise with social responsibility gives something to the community whereas *a Musire enterprise leaves the community with a heritage that lasts for generations, and becomes embodied within it*. While a socially responsible organization can cut aid to the community in times when the enterprise is not doing well, a Musire enterprise suffers in tandem with the community in times of distress.

The leader's ability to be conscious of the needs of a particular nation or institution, moreover, and his or her inner drive and ability to meet those needs, is what builds fair enterprises and democratic nations. Institutional and national peace and prosperity is not achieved by a single heroic effort, for Benjamin, of an individual, but by the collective intellectual effort of all stakeholders.

Goko Routungamiri gEne: Emergence – sacrifice/ selflessness (Kuzvipira)

Leading by giving

The second part of Benjamin's leadership gEne is Sacrifice, giving or self-lessness. In his indigenous Zimbabwean Shona culture, they believe in life after death. Traditionalists believe that the dead can intercede through God (*Mwari*) on their behalf; Christians believe that Jesus Christ can also intercede on behalf of the whole human race. The Shona, moreover, as per tradition, additionally believe that when a person dies he or she will go straight to his ancestors, who would have died before him or her. When the first missionaries came in the late seventeenth century, they convinced people that they no longer needed to ask God to be gracious to them through their ancestors, but now rather through Jesus Christ.

While their forefathers used to conduct sacrifices (*kupira*) using cattle and other small livestock as a means of appeasing ancestors, the Christians believed that Jesus was the ultimate sacrifice for all our sins. So in Shona, the word *kupira* comes from the verb *kupa* (meaning "giving"). *When you give, it means you have sacrificed to remain with less.* In this case, kupira is a process of giving in anticipation of pleasing the dead. When you give to please the living, it is no longer kupira; the Shona call it *kuzvipira* (meaning "we have sacrificed to please the living"). The person who always gives something to others in terms of time, money, assets, food or knowledge is always held in high esteem by the society. People will always say, "*Munhu akanaka uyu anozvipira*" (meaning "he or she is a good person as he/she sacrifices for our benefit"). When the person does this consistently, trust is built between the person and the beneficiaries of that sacrifice.

The unhu of the leader

A leader, for Chasamhuka, then, needs to offer him- or herself as a sacrifice for the common good. In this case, therefore, *kuzvipira* (self-sacrifice) is the second Goko Routungamiri (second gene of leadership). While Westerners, for him, put a lot of emphasis on managers behaving like machines that can be attuned to a style that suits the prevailing environment, African leadership philosophy is woven into the unchanging being (*unhu*) of a leader as some-one who should give up his own pleasures for the common good. The leader should sacrifice his time and resources for his leadership to meet the expected goals of the nation or the enterprise.

In the African context, then, the leader who looks for his or her inter-ests in total neglect of the followers is called "*Ndingoveni*", meaning the one who always looks after his interests in total disregard of the followers' needs and aspirations. Such Africans are children brought up in common trusteeship in African urban or rural communities. The leadership model presented here upholds the supremacy of selfless torchbearers when given the privilege to lead. We now turn to the third *Goko Routungamiri*, that is, to the Communication gEne.

Goko Routungamiri geNe: Navigation – kuzivisana communication

The communicative power of the drumbeat

Communication, third, is as old as life and life is also as old as communi-cation. The origin of life came about by means of communication and the spoken word forms a critical part of Christian religious beliefs. According to Irish psychiatrist and art historian Michael Fitzgerald (2005), interpreting the rock paintings found in the Matobo Hills in Zimbabwe, based on the art of the San, communication started with the beat of the drum:

> The beating of drums in Africa resonates with our spiritual purity and awareness to the coming message. From the drum beat the people will know whether there has been a death and the status of the diseased in that society. The drumbeat will inform the society whether there is an entertainment function or celebration for harvest and fertility.

There is voice in every drumbeat

In contemporary terms, the "shaman", as such, is no longer the traditional cosmologist, so to speak, but rather the knowledge ecologist, information architect or communications technologist. In his article in the *Zimbabwean Herald* of April 2013, Tafadzwa Zimoyo, now turning from rock art to drumming as a means of communication, stated:

> You see, a drum beat is the same as a heartbeat. They have the same pulse, so in that way when we hear the spirit of the drum sound, we then

respond immediately, and in different ways. Remember the first thing you hear when you are born is the heart beat, same with the drum beat. Similarly teamwork involves everyone and motivates them to participate through group work, making a rhythm.

Knowledge and communication

In Shona the word communication, for Benjamin in fact, can be interpreted in various ways, depending on the situation. In a family or community, the word *kuzivisana* means "to enable each other to know". So the core word here is "know", meaning "getting informed". Without the other person informing another, there is no knowledge in existence. What underlies results-driven communication in the practice of *kuzivisana* is the fact that the said communicators are getting reciprocal knowledge.

In Shona, then, the root words, which reinforce communication, are *kuonesana* (getting the team to see from the same angle), *kurangana* (advising each other) and *kutaurirana* (normal conversation). In all these words, the "*ana*" is the root. In other words, the leader-as-communicator must then ensure that whatever activity is taking place is shared and understood by those people with the legitimate right to get it. The communication of knowledge, data and information, then, is the primary constituent of this third part of *relational* leadership. We now turn to the fourth and final element, the genE so to speak, of African leadership.

Goko Routungamiri genE: Effect – *mweya wekukunda* (spirit of success)

The spirit that lives in the body

In Africa there is generally the belief that the real person is not the physical body but the spirit that lives in the body. The spirit, according to Benjamin, finds expression in the person's heart in terms of joy, sorrow, and general feelings towards neighbours, working mates and all humanity. For the Shona people, what drives any person to do or to accomplish any task is then such a spirit in the person. You will often hear a person saying, *ndanga ndichida kuenda kumunda kundosakura asi mweya wangu uri kuramba*, meaning, "*I want to go into the fields to do some weeding but my spirit is not willing.*"

The derivative meaning is that, for a person to be what he or she is in terms of work ethics and sociability, there should be consistent observable behaviour over a long period of time. It is the duty of parents, teachers and other trainers to cultivate good spirits in different fields, be they in community work or politics, in art or science, in education or enterprise, that benefits societies and organizations.

The spirit of success

For anyone to be called a leader, then, he or she needs to have this spirit, *Ane mweya wechakati*, that should be observed by the community or the working group over a prolonged period of time. In deep Shona tradition, this inner invisible soul from within defines the physical person as without, as expressed through words and deeds. It is in this context that any person who is given the role to lead should have the spirit to succeed in that leadership role. Benjamin is not saying that, with that "spirit of winning", success will be guaranteed; he is saying that, with that constant spirit of accomplishment, there is greater probability of success than undertaking a task with the spirit of failure.

Conclusion: the Musire leader – beyond servant leadership

Musire leadership

In his model of African leadership, for Benjamin, then, the leader is more than a "servant leader". He or she must at all times have the inner spirit to accomplish and succeed in whatever undertaking they agree with their people. Such a composite leadership theory transcends transactional, transformational, or servant, leadership, in "western" terms, towards "southern" Musire leadership with these GENE elements: grounding *rhythm*, emergent *selflessness*, navigational *communication* and evoking a spirit of *success.* What gives life to leadership is not the air but the spirit, hence in Shona they breathe *Mweya*, not *mhepo* (meaning "spirit", not "air") It is in this light that the driving force in any leadership is that inner spirit to achieve set goals, objectives and targets.

The tragedy of African leadership philosophy, nationally and organizationally, is that scholars have not taken the time to conceive of, and write up, the theory behind, and context for, such practice, for the world to take note and test this. *A Musire leader, then, is a self-conscious steward who is deeply aware of his immediate relational ecology and the wider ecology set in the enterprise wide or national context.* Moreover, his or her Goko is especially *embodied* in the African rhythm and drumbeat of the south, but it reaches across all the four worlds. The ability to give while not expecting any return from followers is the second Goko of a Musire leader. The ability to inform, inspire and to instruct is related to knowledge, and to communication. It is the ability not only to lend coherence to existing activities, and to activate community, but also to create new knowledge. This is the third Goko of Musire leadership. The spirit to succeed in the face of all kinds of challenges faced is the fourth and final Goko that Benjamin has identified.

Metaphorically in Africa, in the final analysis, when the drum beats everyone responds by dancing, literally or metaphorically, establishing a community circle. In all the four corners of the world they have their own instruments, but what joins us all is the sweetness we get from the rhythm of the beat and the beauty of the dances. In any community, enterprise or nation, when a leader is given the responsibility to lead, he or she must know the people, the systems and the processes needed to complete the responsibility. Success will be realized when the spirit of success is embodied in the followers to accomplish and this applies to national leaders and enterprise leadership.

Overall, then, *bringing in harmony and value is the grounding "dancing" element; the Goko leader emerges as a good person as he/she sacrifices for our benefit; navigating "kuzivisana" means to enable each other to know – without the other person informing another, there is no knowledge existing; by way of effect with the constant spirit of accomplishment, there is greater probability of success than undertaking a task with the spirit of failure.*

Mismatch between theory and practice

Inevitably the question will be asked, why do we fail to see, in most instances, most especially in a political context, the kind of "Musire leadership" to which Benjamin has referred, which he himself has embodied, in Africa? Our integral answer is that the kinds of institutions that have been developed (see Chapter 1 in our previous volume, *Innovation Driven Institutional Research*) have not been GENE-tically evolved out of a local–global heritage, and a dysfunctional mismatch arises. The reason this has happened is that there is no agency to facilitate such a recognition and release of African GENE-ius. In fact, when Benjamin first entered our PhD program, he wanted to model his leadership style, and theoretical orientation, on Winston Churchill!

Further to this, of course, we have the whole backdrop of "northern" colonialism on the one hand, and "southern" parochialism on the other, and instead of fusion between a functional north and south we have a characteristic dysfunctional fission, and its destructive aftermath. To circumvent this, in fact, with a view to embodying individual-and-organizational relational embodiment, we now turn from the personal and communal to the collective institutional engagement with the "calabash of knowledge".

References

Fitzgerald, M. (2005) *The Genesis of Artistic Creativity*. London: Jessica Kingsley Publishers.

Lessem, R. and Schieffer, A. (2009) *Transformation Management: Towards the Integral Enterprise*. Abingdon: Routledge.

Mamukwa, E., Lessem, R. and Schieffer, A. (2014) *Integral Green Zimbabwe: An African Phoenix Rising*. Abingdon: Routledge.

Zimoyo, T. (2013) *Zimbabwean Herald*, 5 April. Harare.

2 Emerging

Calabash – knowledge sharing

Summary of chapter:

1 experiential relational mode of socialized knowing grounded in ubuntu/unhu;
2 emergent imaginal mode of externalized knowing VIA metamorphosis;
3 testing of knowledge conceptually, navigating knowledge combinations;
4 culminating in practical knowing, through internalization.

Introduction: the emergent relational path of embodiment

The indigenous–exogenous challenge

Up to now we have focused on local grounding, and embodiment of integral development, individually and communally in the *relational* "south". We now turn, while still in the relational south, to organizational embodiment in *knowledge sharing*. In the process, we move developmentally from local (grounding) to local–global (emergence), rather than inauthentically leaping from local grounding to global navigation. At the same time, structurally, we turn from learning community to innovation ecosystem.

Authentically and developmentally then, as such, Dr Elizabeth Sarudzai Mamukwa, Human Resource Director currently at Liquid Telecom in Zimbabwe, and formerly at Turnall Holdings, has brought "southern" (African) and "eastern" (Japanese, as we shall see) elements together, emergent wise in local–global organizational knowledge creation, while remaining most strongly connected with the "southern" relational path (Mamukwa *et al.*, 2014).

Zimbabweans, she maintains to begin with, like many indigenous African peoples, have perfected the art of accepting exogenous knowledge by way of navigation – that is, passed from the original colonial masters – including technologies related to such knowledge. In Zimbabwe this phenomenon was exacerbated, historically by colonialism itself, and recently by the skills flight that followed the hyperinflationary era, when people sought working environments with stable currencies as well as friendlier economic conditions. This left many a Zimbabwean organization with huge skills gaps, which often affected capacity utilization. As the culture was to do one's job as instructed, serious skills gaps were experienced when specific employees left organizations.

The challenge then for Mamukwa was to build on traditional approaches in Africa to the transfer of knowledge, and extend this to incorporate the creation of new knowledge. The starting point was to build confidence in the African people so that they came to believe in themselves. They needed to see themselves in relation to their local village, as it were, as Benjamin intimated in our opening chapter, as equals in this global village, equals with the capacity to make a meaningful contribution to knowledge, in their African-ness. This brings us to the *Calabash*.

Cooperative inquiry lodged within an innovation ecosystem

The *Calabash of Knowledge*, as Mamukwa has termed it, is the result of an action research project, via so-called *cooperative inquiry* (Heron, 1996) that she carried out when she was Human Resource Director at Turnall Holdings, a manufacturing company in Harare. The inspiration for this research with a view to innovation, apart from fulfilling the requirements of her PhD program in Integral Development, was her experience of the result of the crippling of industry from a skills perspective, following the skills flight in Zimbabwe as a result of a harsh economic environment, particularly between 2003 and 2009. The idea was to come up with an innovation that would enhance the learning orientation of her organization as a whole and promote knowledge transfer, as well as the improvement and the outright creation of new knowledge.

Cooperative inquiry (CI), then, the brainchild of British research philosopher and developmental psychologist John Heron, in the 1990s, involved Mamukwa's inquiry group, her community circle so to speak, in four modes of knowing, which in fact are analogous to our own integral rhythm and, as we shall see, as well as to Nonaka and Taheuchi's (1995) knowledge creating spiral. "Western" intentional action, for Heron then

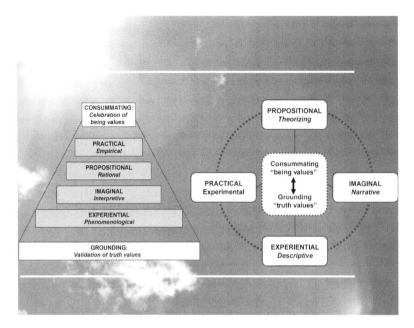

Figure 2.1 The four modes of knowing

(see Figure 2.1), *at the apex of the supportive pyramid of fourfold knowing, consummates it and brings it to an integrated focal point.* Undertaken by a group of co-inquirers, it becomes a concerted and congruent set of behaviours that is honed through cyclical integration of all four modes, experiential and imaginal, propositional and practical, and includes that integration as a necessary condition of its continuing practice. In fact, and in line with our innovation ecosystem (introduced in our second volume, *Awakening Integral Consciousness*), practice is aligned with facilitation, conceptualization with research, imagination with catalyzation and experience with stewardship.

What is below, then, grounds and validates what is above, and what is above consummates, celebrates and shows forth what is below.

Practice, then, crowns the world with the value of human flourishing. Valid outcomes alone are not enough. They need to be self-transcending and metamorphose into exuberant outcomes. As such, while Mamukwa herself then played a *catalytic* role, and her CEO was the project *steward*, and the inquirers themselves the *co-researchers*, the production coordinator was the *facilitator* of knowledge sharing and implementation.

How the calabash of knowledge creation came into being

Why, then, in a Zimbabwean African context, was the metaphor of the cala-bash used? The calabash was among one of the first plants to be cultivated in the world. Although it is edible, it was not cultivated for its culinary qualities but rather for its use as a container, a musical instrument, a bottle or a pipe. In Africa the big calabash is used mostly as a container for water, beer or other non-alcoholic drink such as *maheu* (an opaque drink made out of fermented maize meal). The smaller size is used as a drinking cup (*mukombe*), and for sharing drink and water. Medium sizes can be used as food containers. The calabash can also be used as a musical instrument (*hosho*) to bring rhythmic harmony to any situation.

One can easily imagine the rhythm forming a harmonic sound with the sound of the machines of the factory. The metaphoric rhythm is further accentuated by the fact that the cycle of knowledge is not necessarily by project, but ongoing, day in and day out, whether there is a project happen-ing or not. It should ideally become a way of life at the workplace if the enterprise claims to be a learning organization. By extension, if this rhythm is instilled in the people at work, what is to say that they cannot spread this to their homes and villages?

The calabash of knowledge creation as an offspring of CI and SECI

The focus on relationships: ubuntu/unhu

The metaphorical calabash is designed in the shape of a real calabash, and is specifically then divided into five spheres, which will be explained below. The Calabash of Knowledge Creation is an offspring of Nonaka and Takeuchi's (1995) SECI (Socialization, Externalization, Combination, Internalization) model, if not also of Heron's four modes of knowing (underlined), the former cited in our previous work on *Awakening integral consciousness*, combined with our *Integral Worlds* (*southern* experiential Socialization / *eastern* imaginal Externalization / *northern* propositional/ conceptual Combination / *western* practical Internalization) with three major modifications.

The first one, for Mamukwa, is that, in the Calabash, *relationships are central to the whole concept of knowledge transfer as well as the crea-tion of new knowledge. Such relationships must be appropriate in the*

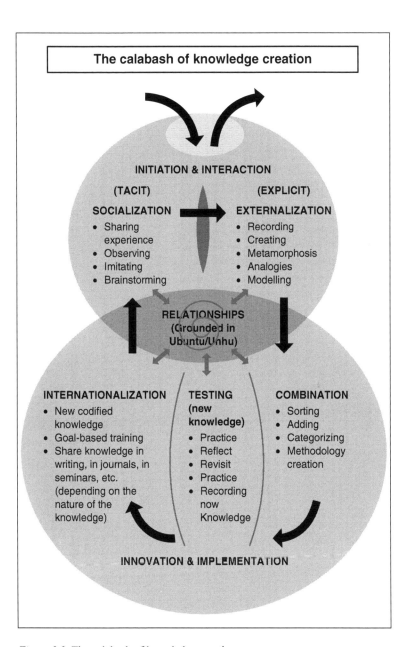

Figure 2.2 The calabash of knowledge creation

African sense, and must be grounded in community values of Ubuntu/Unhu. Problems at work, in the community and in any other situation, bind us together. The societal imbalances are at the core of the forces that push us to want to see change. This results in developing a common cause, and we end up working together to come up with a common solution. Consequently, in all the spheres of the Calabash, people continue to work together to come up with some kind of consensus. Knowledge creation in this respect, then, is more of a collaborative than an individual activity or phenomenon.

Knowledge is highly interactive

The second modification is the issue of testing new knowledge for authenticity before it can be classified as such and before it can be officially passed on to other people. The testing comes before internalization/internationalization because it is pertinent that correct, proven knowledge that is credible and has integrity is internalized and internationalized. If any prospective new knowledge fails the test, it must ideally be thrown out at this stage, and the process started all over again.

The third modification is the opening at the top of the calabash, which implies that knowledge is highly interactive. It must be allowed to go in and out of the calabash – shared with other people. We should therefore always be prepared to share our knowledge, and be open to working with

Table 2.1 Knowledge rhythms

Embodying Integral Development: Relational Emergence *Calabash of knowledge creation* Knowledge rhythms: socializing, externalizing, testing, internalizing

- *Attributes of embodiment* – RELATIONAL PATH: <u>Grounding</u> – Goko personal and communal engagement; <u>Emergence</u> – *calabash of group knowledge sharing*; <u>Navigation</u> – GENE rhythm of social innovation; <u>Effect</u> – integral realities/societal transformation. RENEWAL PATH: <u>Grounding</u> – integral state; <u>Emergence</u> – institutional integration; <u>Navigation</u> – releasing GENE-ius; <u>Effect</u> – societal renaissance. REASONED REALIZATION PATH: <u>Grounding</u> – school education for all the senses; <u>Emergence</u> – enterprise learning and development; <u>Navigation</u> – sustainable development university; <u>Effecting</u> – institutional genealogy.
- *Integrator role*: embodied leader, e.g. **Elizabeth Sarudzai Mamukwa**.
- *Rhythmical GENE of knowledge creation*: experiential relational mode of **socialized** knowing *grounded* in **ubuntu/unhu**; emergent imaginal mode of **externalized** knowing arising through **metamorphosis**; followed by **testing** of knowledge conceptually and propositionally, thereby navigating knowledge **combinations**; culminating in **practical** knowing, through **internalization**, so you know where you are going, and what you effect.

knowledge from other sources. The Calabash of Knowledge Creation is presented above.

Conclusion: Harambe – working together

A lot can happen when several people come together to tackle a problem that concerns all of them, as Mamukwa experienced in the development of the Calabash of Knowledge Creation through the Turnall action research group, *Denhe re Ruzivo*. In these processes of research and development, she discovered that a societal problem only remains as such before the people affected have made up their minds to confront and tame it. The process of coming up with a solution can be a very fulfilling one in terms of bonding and strengthening relationships, but more importantly, for empowering people and making them realize that they have the capacity to solve the problems at hand.

Through the Calabash of Knowledge Creation it was possible to resolve the skills challenges in Mamukwa's organization, with the help of the people within Turnall Holdings. Mamukwa also learned that nature has the solutions to our problems and challenges, from the calabash to termites. If only we could take the trouble to find those solutions in the right places. Overall then, as such, and through relationally embodying integral knowledge rhythms, *the experiential relational mode of socialized knowing was grounded in ubuntu/unhu; the emergent imaginal mode of externalized knowing arose through metamorphosis; this was followed by testing of knowledge conceptually and propositionally, thereby navigating knowledge combinations; culminating in practical knowing, through internalization, so you know where you are going, and what you effect.*

In the event, and as of 2015, Mamukwa in fact left her former company, Turnall Holdings, as indeed did Benjamin (his company was part of the multinational SABMiller, which in 2016 is in the course of being taken over by the Belgian headquartered AB InBev multinational). The innovation ecosystem she had established in the company was thereby dissipated. Supposedly this is because, for all their individual and organizational efforts, the corporate form that their enterprises constitute, and the state of the Zimbabwean, if not also South African, nations as a whole, were not sufficiently congruent with their efforts, to altogether embody such integral personal and communal, organizational and societal development. We now therefore turn, while still on the southern, relational path, from grounding and emergence to navigation, and as such, explicitly, towards social innovation via our GENE rhythm as a whole.

References

Heron, J. (1996) *Cooperative Inquiry: Research into the Human Condition*. London: Sage.

Mamukwa, E., Lessem, R. and Schieffer, A. (2014) *Integral Green Zimbabwe: A Phoenix Rising from the Ashes*. Abingdon: Routledge.

Nonaka, I. and Takeuchi, H. (1995) *The Knowledge Creating Company: How Japanese Companies Create the Dynamics of Innovation*. New York: Oxford University Press.

3 Navigating

GENE rhythm – social innovation

Summary of chapter:

1   grounding basic research – immerse yourselves in a natural communal
    context;
2   emerging through applied research – probe into a unique life world;
3   navigate by design, giving voice to the marginalized/decolonizing
    your minds;
4   undertake collective action, developing self and community-integral
    innovation.

Introduction: relational navigation/integral institutional embodiment

Why social falls behind technological innovation

We now turn, socially and *relationally*, to the Embodiment of integral
development, institutionally, with a focus on research and innovation,
thereby serving to bring about emancipatory navigation. We thereby arrive
at a greater degree of social abstraction than was hitherto the case with
Goko leadership, and knowledge rhythms, albeit that we retain our relational orientation. In the process we focus on *social innovation*, following
upon knowledge creation, and relational leadership, thereby also aligned
with our inter-institutional genealogy, with a view to accomplishing innovation driven, institutional research.

In fact, while technological innovation forever gathers pace, most visibly today in the ICT field, so-called *social innovation* remains left out in
the cold, or at most receives only lip service, so that social business, entrepreneurship and innovation are seen as virtually interchangeable. There is,
in our view then, no newly substantive economic or enterprise foundation,
emerging in practice, and indeed there is no ontological (theory of reality)

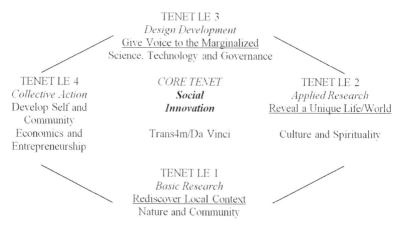

Figure 3.1 Embodying relational effect: social innovation

emancipation from the old economic and enterprise forms. There is, then, a virtually complete absence of any fundamental transformation, of structure and process, in economy and enterprise. Why is this so?

Technological, by way of comparison with social, innovation, at least in the industrialized world, is well established, conceptually and institutionally, most particularly in America. University-based research departments, in the natural sciences, corporate research laboratories and government-sponsored ones, separately or altogether, have small or large teams engaged in such scientific or technological innovation. Whether we are talking of the discovery of DNA, scientifically, or of the development of the internet, technologically, public, private and civic institutions have been majorly involved. The situation is totally different in the social sciences and the humanities, where neither such research teams, with their massive budgets, nor an explicit research-to-innovation process – from basic to applied research on to development and commercialization – has been established.

In fact, research in the social sciences is generally conducted by isolated individuals, and a path from research to, in this case, *social*, or indeed *socio-economic*, innovation, has not been explicitly evolved.

In fact, with the onset of proliferating unemployment and social as well as economic injustice, people all over the world tend to look towards politicians, if not also to the business community (and occasionally to civil society), to address these burning issues. But where are the universities, where are the social science research establishments, in relation to this?

Indeed the single notable, today somewhat notorious, exception to this rule of omission has been the one and only Chicago School of Economics,

Table 3.1 Institutionalized social innovation

Embodying Integral Development: Relational Navigation   *Social innovation: origination to transformation*   Basic and applied social research, design and innovation
• *Attributes of embodiment* – RELATIONAL PATH: <u>Grounding</u> – Goko personal and communal engagement; <u>Emergence</u> – calabash of group knowledge sharing; <u>Navigation</u> – ***GENE rhythm of social innovation***; <u>Effect</u> – integral realities/societal transformation. RENEWAL PATH: <u>Grounding</u> – integral State; <u>Emergence</u> – institutional integration; <u>Navigation</u> – releasing GENE-ius; <u>Effect</u> – societal renaissance. REASONED REALIZATION PATH: <u>Grounding</u> – school education for all the senses; <u>Emergence</u> – enterprise learning and development; <u>Navigation</u> – sustainable development university; <u>Effecting</u> – institutional genealogy.   • *Integrator role*: e.g., ***Trans4m, Da Vinci Institute***.   • *Integral relational innovation*: *Grounding and basic research* – immerse yourselves in a natural communal context and ***rediscover your local context****; emerging through applied research* – probe into a unique life world *and* ***reveal its local/global meaning***; *navigate by design* through giving voice to the marginalized and ***decolonizing your minds***; *undertake collective action, **developing self and community*** by way of integral innovation.

where the late Milton Friedman had been based. The School, over the past four decades, had an inordinate influence on the spread of neo-liberal economics throughout the world, often in very shady circumstances, as for example had been the case in Pinochet's Chile. As such it had well-funded teams of social scientists, all working out of a similar neo-liberal ethos, whereby "economic man" prevailed over all else, and they had a very definite practical influence over politicians and economists worldwide. Yet they have been very much the exception rather than the rule, and arguably have in fact preserved the status quo, while claiming to be reformers and economic revolutionaries! So where do we go from here?

Towards societal renewal

The functional means towards that socio-economic end is, as we shall see, *social* research and innovation, via, structurally, sanctuary, university and laboratory. As such we evolve local identity towards global integrity, rather than "thinking global – acting local", that is, a travesty of the integral truth. We start here, then, with social innovation, as a process of such "integral" research and development, building on the social sciences and humanities generally, and then move on to the specifically socio-economic substance that underlies it. Finally we shall turn to the structural reconfiguration needed.

Social innovation as a process

Local identity to global integrity

We begin, then, by focusing on the process of research and innovation, from a specifically socio-economic perspective, albeit in relation to the different cultures, and societies, in which we are engaged – most specifically, in this case, in Southern Africa. Our partner on this journey, as such, is the Da Vinci Institute in South Africa, co-founded by Nelson Mandela in the 1990s, and focused on the management of technology, from a social and economic perspective.

According to our *integral worlds*, or "worldviews" (see our previous volume, *Awakening Integral Consciousness*), by way of what we consider to be a necessary shorthand, we have identified four major, culturally laden realities or worldviews (Lessem *et al.*, 2012), already indicated, as southern – *humanistic*; eastern – *holistic*; northern – *rational*; and western – *pragmatic*. This differentiation, and subsequent integration, we consider necessary, if we are to operate, socio-economically, with what we term local identity and *global integrity* (Lessem and Schieffer, 2009b).

Global integrity to social innovation

In each of our "worlds", moreover, there is a potential path of *social* innovation (see Table 3.2 below), in fact from origination (basic research) to transformation (integral innovation), via foundation and emancipation, as yet largely unrealized. Our pre-emphasis, as illustrated in bold, is with the *relational* "south" here, though a country like South Africa will also have strong "northern" and "western" if not also "eastern" attributes.

We call the four such paths the *relational* (humanistic) path, the holistic path of *renewal*, the rational path of *reason*, and the pragmatic path of *realization*, in this work here combining the "north-west" (Lessem and Schieffer, 2009a). Each path tends to favour one branch of the social sciences over another, for example business and economics is the path of "western" realization.

In addition, every path has a particular emphasis, for example that of "healing nature and community" for the functional "southern" relational path. Most importantly, though, each path has an integral trajectory, equivalent to that in the natural sciences, from fundamental research to commercialization – or transformative action in the social arena – ultimately constituting innovation, for us. We shall now illustrate the composite of paths for each phase, that is, from origination to transformation, in turn.

In Table 3.2 below, then, we have set out the process of social innovation, as we see it, for each of our four paths, from origination (grounding)

Table 3.2 Integral socio-economic innovation

S	E	N	W
Humanistic ***RELATIONAL PATH***	*Holistic PATH OF RENEWAL*	*Rational PATH OF REASON*	*Pragmatic PATH OF REALIZATION*
Ecology **Anthropology**	Psychology Philosophy	Sociology Political Science	Economics Business
Heal nature/ ***community***	*Cultural renaissance*	*Establish an opportunity*	*Create open society*
Being: Origination – Basic Research – Grounding			
Immerse yourselves in a natural/ communal context	Rediscover your cultural heritage	Construct a socio-economic theory	Apply a novel business idea
Becoming: Foundation – Applied Research – Emergence			
Probe into unique life world	Reveal the local/ global meaning	Imaginatively develop hypotheses	Learn from/ adapt to experience
Knowing: Emancipation – Design and Development – Navigation			
Give voice to the marginalized	Liberate the oppressed	Decolonise the mind	Challenge the socio-economic system
Doing : Transformation – Socio-economic Innovation – Effect			
Undertake collective action	Develop self, organization, society	Establish a democratic design	Promote initiative/ reflect

to transformation (effect). Thereafter we shall consider each such phase, process wise, from first basic, second applied, research, to third development and ultimately integral innovation, in turn. We highlight, moreover and in each case, in bold, the southern path that most concerns us here.

While the innovation paths extend from the relational to realization, the corresponding lead disciplines (anthropology to economics), and the overall socio-economic aspirations (healing communities to creating opportunities), follow thereafter. We start then with basic research, in the social sciences, alongside origination, ontologically and grounding, <u>G</u>ene-ius. At this point, moreover, in terms of embodying integral development, and in relation to our *integral rounds*, we are operating at an organizational and societal level.

Basic research to commercializing integral innovation

Basic research – origination: grounding innovation

Whereas in the natural sciences, the *origination* or indeed *grounding* of innovation takes place through *basic* research in, say, physics, chemistry or biology, in the social sciences it is lodged, for us, in a basic human *Mode* or basic research Method that is,

- a *Being* mode – <u>descriptive</u> method (humanistic – southern), or
- a *Becoming* mode – <u>narrative</u> method (holistic – becoming), or alternately
- a *Knowing* mode – method of <u>theorizing</u> (rational – northern), or finally
- a *Doing* mode – <u>experimental</u> method (pragmatic – western).

We elaborate on this in Table 3.3 below, with the relational path in bold:

These, in effect, are generally and exclusively identified as basic <u>methods</u> of social research, and are thereby conventionally bereft of any hint of ultimate innovation, because of their characteristically analytical, and individualistic nature and scope. Moreover, they are *conventionally disconnected from any underlying human modality, the four altogether, being and becoming, knowing and doing in our terms, serving to bring about global integrity.* We now review such <u>method</u> with integrity, that is for each of the four paths, duly aligned with *basic* research. Ultimately, we shall position this, that is, basic research-as-origination, within an

Table 3.3 Research origination: basic research

S	E	N	W
BEING: **Humanistic** **RELATIONAL PATH**	*BECOMING*: *Holistic PATH* *OF RENEWAL*	*KNOWING*: *Rational PATH* *OF REASON*	*DOING*: *Pragmatic* *PATH OF* *REALIZATION*
Ecology **Anthropology**	Psychology History/ Philosophy	Sociology Political Science	Economics Business
Heal nature/ **community**	*Cultural* *renaissance*	*Establish an open* *society*	*Create* *opportunity*
Origination – Basic Research – Grounding			
Immerse **yourselves in a** **disrupted cultural** **context** *Describing*	Rediscover your cultural heritage *Narrating*	Construct a socio-economic theory *Theorizing*	Apply a novel idea *Experimenting*

integral trajectory, from basic research to social innovation. Such a process is ultimately *integral* to the extent that it follows a stratified trajectory, from primary or pre-conceptual, being and becoming, to secondary, conceptual knowing and post-conceptual doing.

Specifically for us, then, *basic* research is a means of origination, in the social sciences, with a view to social innovation, thereby achieving desired ends. By initial way of local grounding, then, you individually/collectively, with a particular focus in our *southern* case (underlined) on immersion,

- *immerse* yourself in a disrupted natural and communal context (describe);
- *rediscover* your unfolding cultural heritage (narrate);
- *construct* a socio-economic theory that builds on both (theorize);
- *apply* a novel idea, building on heritage, addressing disruption (experiment).

As far as such innovation, as opposed to mere research method in isolation, is ultimately and *integrally* concerned, this is the begining rather than the end of the story, whereby the whole research–innovation trajectory is, as we shall see, integral. Indeed, this can be compared and contrasted with typical social research, whether market, consumer or morale based, where it ends just there!

Research spread across *integral worlds*, for us, then, involves all four worlds, and *integral* research-and-*innovation*, as we shall see, *rhythmically*, extends from origination (grounding) to transformation (effecting). Indeed, and by way of analogy with technological innovation, origination conforms with basic research, and transformation with ultimate innovation, applied research (foundation) and development (emancipation) lies in between.

We now turn from basic to applied research, in relation to each of our four paths, worlds, and indeed now foundations.

Applied research – foundation: emerging innovation

It has been widely assumed, in social and economic research, around the world, that the so-called *empirical* approach is the hallmark of "scientific research". The stock approach to identifying "independent and dependent variables", thereby analyzing linear cause and effect, has been central to such a thereby empirically based orientation. In fact, and ironically, we have found in the "developing world", that such an empirical orientation among students is that most vigorously pursued by academics, and most poorly followed by those at the receiving end, totally unaware of this "western" imposition.

As such, learning from empirically laden, directly observable events and experiences, becomes the order of what we term the "western" day. Yet for us, in terms of our *integral realities*, this is only one of at least four different research foundations, a "western" one so to speak, underlying a pragmatic path of realization. Altogether then, for us, there are four such emerging foundations, or worldviews, of which "empiricism" (pragmatic) is only one; the other three are phenomenological (humanistic in bold, see Table 3.4 below), interpretive (holistic) and rational in turn. Moreover, we align these with applied research, in the natural sciences, in that each is applied to, or emerges out of, a particular context.

So, for example, *if I am doing "research" into the use of mobile phones, in a "southern" relational culture, I should be drawing upon a phenomenological foundation, whereby I connect mobile communications with the foundational, convivial "life world" of the people* with (not *on*) whom I am doing the research. Research foundations then involve, alternately,

- *engaging* with a unique part the life world plays in a whole (phenomenological);
- *revealing* the meaning of the local in the light of the global (interpretive);
- *establishing*, imaginatively, new hypotheses (rational); as well as finally
- *learning* from, and adapting to experience (empirical).

Such applied, foundational integrity links the local with the global, the indigenous with the exogenous, so that such a foundation, in each of the four cases, is built on solid ground, in two complementary respects. First, it draws

Table 3.4 Research foundation: applied research

S	E	N	W
Humanistic RELATIONAL PATH	*Holistic PATH OF RENEWAL*	*Rational PATH OF REASON*	*Pragmatic PATH OF REALIZATION*
Ecology Anthropology	Psychology Philosophy	Sociology Political Science	Economics Business
Heal nature/ community	*Cultural renaissance*	*Establish an open society*	*Create opportunity*
Foundation – Applied Research – Emergence			
Engage in unique life world	*Reveal* the local/ global meaning	Imaginatively *establish* new hypotheses	*Learn* from/adapt to experience
Phenomenological	*Interpretive*	*Rational*	*Empirical*

on the specifics of a particular community, culture, science and enterprise. Second, those narrow, albeit deeply set, specifics are married up with a broadly based, social scientific – phenomenological, interpretive, rational and empirical – generality. For example, having richly and concretely described what we see, as a committed layperson, or even as an unusually well-attuned market researcher, in a community project on the ground, say in Chinyika in rural Zimbabwe, we then need to reflect on the particular life worlds of the Karanga and Baremba people therein, from a more scholarly, though still particularist, anthropological or ecological perspective.

We now turn from origination and foundation to emancipation.

Navigate innovation – emancipation: design/development

We are now at a turning point, on the cusp, if you like, between research and impending innovation, the "tipping point" whereby we turn to our so-called "navigation", or more specifically, to *emancipation*. Why, then, does emancipation, as research *and* development, pave the way for integral innovation?

Our overall argument, at this point, is that developed and developing societies alike, though more distinctly the latter, are generally not "emancipated", in that their economic if not also socio-political frameworks – self-concepts and organizational institutions – do not measure up to the combination of who they are (grounding) and what they have become (emerging) in relation to others (see for example Chapter 2). In developing societies, this is typically the case because locals have been too long dominated, from within and without, by others (external colonizers, internal dictators, composite experts and elites) to "know" who and what they intrinsically are.

Table 3.5 Emancipatory research: development

S	E	N	W
Humanistic RELATIONAL PATH	*Holistic PATH OF RENEWAL*	*Rational PATH OF REASON*	*Pragmatic PATH OF REALIZATION*
Ecology Anthropology	Psychology Philosophy	Sociology Political Science	Economics Business
Heal nature/ community	*Cultural renaissance*	*Establish an open society*	*Create opportunity*
Emancipation – Design and Development – Navigation			
Give voice to the marginalized Feminism	*Liberate the oppressed Critical theory*	*Decolonize the mind Postmodernism*	*Challenge the socio-economic system Critical realism*

This is exacerbated by the fact that nation-states in Africa, the Middle East and Asia, had been "cobbled together", in colonial times, out of disparate groups, without having purposefully engaged in "healing" or "making whole" the divides between them. We can see then, highlighted in bold in Table 3.5 above, where this leads us, emancipation and navigation wise.

In the developed world the same applies, even if to a lesser extent, in that our economic concepts and institutions, throughout the industrialized world, are dominated by those of the UK and America, whether we live, for example, in Germany, Japan or the Czech Republic. Moreover, in the US itself, the "west" (Anglo-Saxon), if not also the "north" (German, Dutch and Scandinavian), has hitherto dominated over the "rest" (African, Hispanic and Asian–American). So that lack of integral development prevents the world at large, ourselves included, from, in emancipatory research (in brackets) guise:

- *giving* voice to the culturally, socially, economically marginalized (feminism);
- *liberating* the politically and economically oppressed (critical theory);
- *decolonizing* the mind (post-modernism); and
- *challenging* the prevailing economic and social system (critical realism).

Though the emancipatory critiques, in research terms, are little known in general social science, and certainly everyday, circles, all are critical of the status quo. As such, "social revolution" is a prerequisite for development, or indeed metamorphosis: thereby *emancipation*. In fact, the very reason that "reactive" revolution is called for, and is an all too often, sadly, bloody business, as we now see in the Middle East, is because of a lack of "proactive" research (basic origination and applied foundation), development, and ultimate innovation.

In other words, *local Origination (basic research), as per one or other relevant human mode, and a local–global Foundation (applied research) have not been pursued, to form the basis for a newly global Emancipation* (research *and* development) and ultimately global–local societal transformation (integral innovation). We finally turn to such transformation, and ultimately integral, research and now innovation.

Integral innovation – transform: effect innovation

At this culminating stage, from social research to innovation, from origination to transformation, we turn from grounding to effect. As ultimate "commercialization" has purely economic, as opposed to combined socioeconomic connotations, we refer to ultimate, and now social *innovation*

Table 3.6 Transformative research-and-innovation

S	E	N	W
Humanistic **RELATIONAL** **PATH**	*Holistic* *PATH OF* *RENEWAL*	*Rational* *PATH OF* *REASON*	*Pragmatic* *PATH OF* *REALIZATION*
Ecology **Anthropology**	Psychology Philosophy	Sociology Political Science	Economics Business
Heal nature/ **community**	*Cultural* *renaissance*	*Establish an* *open society*	*Create* *opportunity*
Transformation – Socioeconomic Activation – Effect			
Undertake **collective action**	*Co-evolve* self, organization, society	*Develop* a democratic design	*Initiate* action/ reflection
Participatory **Action Research**	*Co-operative* *Inquiry*	*Socio-Technical* *Design*	*Action* *Research*

instead, thereby combining, accumulatively and thereby integrally, origination, foundation, emancipation and transformation.

• you *undertake* collective action (participatory action research);
• you *co-evolve* self and community, organization and society (cooperative inquiry);
• you *develop* a democratic organizational design (socio-technical design);
• you *initiate* and reflect (action research).

This completes the socio-economic research-and-innovation *process*, from basic and then applied research to development and then integral innovation, whereby emancipation provides the bridge, between research and innovation. We also, incidentally, disciplinary wise, have encompassed the full range, from anthropology and ecology, or geography, at one end of the continuum, to business, or management, and economics at the other.

We are now ready to conclude.

Conclusion: beyond new wine in old bottles

Integral innovation not gut reaction

The root problem, for us at this emancipatory point, is that there is no tradition, or institutionalization, of social innovation, as a means of navigating our way through development. Moreover, such innovation needs to be differentiated, as well as ultimately integrated, in two forms. First, it needs to be culturally differentiated. Enterprise in the "south", as in Zimbabwe or Nigeria, needs to be profoundly differentiated from that, for example, in the "west". Second, reality needs to be stratified. As American philosopher Ken Wilber (2006) tells us, we do not live in "flatlands". We have therefore distinguished, in the course of developing a knowledge-based social economy, between origination (basic research), foundation (applied research), emancipation (development) and transformation (innovation), in the socio-economic domain.

We need to plumb the depths

If, therefore, we are to resolve such thorny problems as those of poverty and injustice, climate change and the ravages of closed societies, like for example Syria hitherto, we have to plumb the depths, in each worldly case. It is not enough to "originate" a new form of enterprise, say the "social" enterprise. Such a new enterprise needs a substantively new foundation, or functioning; it requires radical emancipation from prevailing structures and processes; and ultimately there is a need for full-scale transformation. To say that socialism has failed, and therefore we need to retain one or another form of capitalism, for us integrally speaking, just won't wash. Such an approach will never reach the great unwashed! There is no emancipation. No transformation. Just adaptation.

To bring about such ultimate, social transformation, then, we need people and institutions that focus on social, not merely technological – albeit supplemented by systems and focused on people – innovation. We need the equivalent of Edison's Menlo Park in the social and economic arena, and we need such culturally differentiated, and ontologically stratified, institutions in all four corners of the globe. We don't have the daily survival problems to deal with that beset the "developing" world. That said, at the time of writing, in the summer of 2011, there are riots in the streets of London. So we in the "global south" need to set a new example.

Towards an inter-institutional genealogy

Now we come to the structural crunch, and an odd one at that. We shall be reiterating later (see Chapter 11) the *Inter-Institutional Genealogy* that we first introduced in the previous volume, *Innovation Driven Institutional Research*, subsequent to our *Integral Dynamics* (Schieffer and Lessem, 2012). This form of evolved university is the means we have conceived, but to date only partially realized, for Embodying Integral Development. As such we have alluded, separately and together, to a community, sanctuary, research academy and laboratory.

We now turn from *relationally* based social innovation, embodying organizational and societal development, to fully fledged societal transformation, following our integral realms: natural and cultural, social and economic, in turn.

References

Lessem, R. and Schieffer, A. (2009a) *Integral Research and Innovation*. Farnham: Gower Publishing.

Lessem, R. and Schieffer, A. (2009b) *Transformation Management: Toward the Integral Enterprise*. Farnham: Gower Publishing.

Lessem, R., Muchineripi, P. and Kada, S. (2012) *Integral Community: Political Economy to Social Commons*. Abingdon: Routledge.

Schieffer, A. and Lessem, R. (2012) *Integral Development: Developing Self and Organisation, Community and Society*. Farnham: Gower Publishing.

Wilber, K. (2006) *Integral Spirituality: A Startling New Role for Religion in the Modern and Postmodern World*. Boston, MA: Integral Books.

4   Effecting

Integral realities – societal transformation

Summary of chapter:

1   grounded in nature and community – community building functionally aligned with environmentalism societally;
2   emerging through culture and spirituality via conscious evolution functionally aligned with culturalism societally;
3   navigating through science and technology via knowledge creation functionally aligned with social democracy societally;
4   effected through economics and finance via sustainable development functionally aligned with overall sustainability societally, creating a world without poverty.

Introduction: the relational path to effecting integral development

Turning conventional wisdom on its head

In our *relational* grounding, emerging and navigating our way, in the previous three chapters, towards the effective embodiment of integral development, personally and communally, organizationally and societally, we turn the conventional world upside down, by implying that it is the role of ultimately what we have termed an inter-institutional *genealogy* (see Chapter 11) to perform such navigation, rather than that of politicians, captains of industry, or even business or social entrepreneurs. They have instead a major role to play, as we shall now see, in *effecting* rather than navigating development. Indeed, in this chapter on embodying integral development, we turn from organizational and communal, to effecting societal development.

In that context, to begin with, at a micro level, an integral enterprise (Lessem and Schieffer, 2009) – for us community building, consciously evolving, knowledge creating, and developing sustainably as such – needs an integral society in which to thrive. In fact, in Chapter 8, we shall be illustrating such a would-be integral society, in effect that of Oman.

The vision of an integral society: from twofold to fourfold

Our fourfold *integral worlds* approach – part and parcel of *Awakening Integral Consciousness*, as we saw in volume 2 of this series – builds on an integral perspective of society as well as of enterprise. As such we reject the conventionally twofold divisions between capitalism and socialism, north and south, or east and west, industry and academe, as being static and divisive, rather than dynamic and inclusive, worldly wise. Indeed, the original development of human communities and societies followed a fourfold rhythm. Tens of thousands of years ago, when the first human communities were forged, they formed a deep and immediate relationship with nature. It was only much later, that cultural artefacts were added to such communities, initially most likely through burial rites. From there communities started to organize themselves more systematically, and developed initial simple structures, roles and positions. Thereafter it took a long time, until such communities started engaging in trade with other communities.

These initial differentiations mirror, to this day, the core life-giving functions of human communities, enterprises and societies: a "southern" enterprise function of *community building* focused societally on nature and community through environmentalism; an "eastern" such function of *conscious evolution* focusing on culture and spirituality through what might be termed culturalism; a northern enterprise function of *knowledge creation* focusing on systematic knowledge (science), technology, and governance

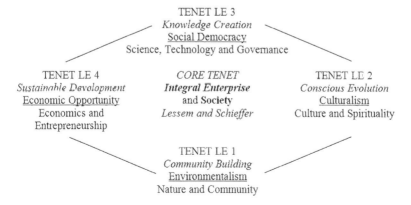

Figure 4.1 Relational effect of embodiment: *enterprise*/society

structures, in the context of <u>social democracy</u>; and a western function of *sustainable development* focusing on economics (including trade), finance, and <u>creating economic opportunity</u>.

Public and private sectors versus integral society

With a view to promoting an Integral Society (Lessem *et al.*, 2014), then, we ask the overall question: to what extent can new economic and societal frameworks be informed by such an integral perspective? Let's meanwhile recall the status quo. The conventional perspective sees "business and society" as twofold – business *and* society. The first, that is, business or the "private" sector, in our globalizing and privatizing age, generally today takes precedence over society, conventionally understood as the "public sector". Usually, business and society, private and public enterprise remain separate from one another, though they may share common stakeholders. In recent decades, moreover, a new societal force has emerged, called "civic society", cited by Philippine social activist Nicanor Perlas (2003) as "the most important social innovation of the 20th century".

Perlas, one of the key proponents of an alternative approach to globalization and internationally recognized – winning the Right Livelihood Award – builds on the threefold perspective on society of his late mentor, Austria's Rudolf Steiner. For Steiner (1977), the twofold division of society is replaced by a *threefold commonwealth*, incorporating now public (political–governmental), private (economic–business) and civic (cultural–communal) realms of activity. The civic sector, however, is generally seen in opposition to business, partly also in opposition to the public sector. In short, the civic sector seems to act as a kind of "correcting force" within society, challenging conventional practices of the business and the public sector. In recent years, though, the three sectors started to move from opposing each other to various forms of public–civic–private partnerships. Our inter-institutional genealogy follows that trend.

This seems to be a step in the right direction, as no single sector can itself address the complexity of today's challenges. However, as we see it, such partnership does not go far enough, partly because it does not explicitly involve the "animate" – environmental – dimension (see Chapter 2 in *Innovation Driven Institutional Research*, referring to the fourfold Sekem Group as a *sustainable community in the Egyptian desert*). What we have done in our *Integral Worlds* approach is that we have *introduced a "fourfold organism". Explicitly, we have added an "animate", environmental dimension or sector, both at a micro and a macro level*. What, then, does this actually mean?

The integral fourfold process dynamically balances what are potentially opposites: so sustainable economic development, materially, and conscious evolution of the spirit, for example, serve to balance out, rather than exclude, one another. In this way, each of our four elements reinforces one another, in a virtuous circle, or indeed vital spiral.

Fission rather than fusion

If we then reflect on the macro forces prevailing today, what we observe, to a significant degree, is a kind of splitting, or fragmentation, as we see for example in the Brexit case in the UK (as at the time of writing in November 2016) that promotes independence rather than interdependence. In fact, in the forefront of this trend are economic forces of globalization, which dominate all else (this is what gave rise to Marxism in the twentieth century and, arguably, to Islamicism in the twenty-first). On the whole, though, *because the micro-organism is set within the wider context of the macro-organism, the former is ultimately dependent upon the latter.* So during the 1990s when economic materialism, under the neo-liberal Anglo-Saxon ascendancy of the time, reached its greatest heights, the fusion of "Japanese Spirit/Western Technique", which heralded the Japanese communitarian economic miracle, was torn apart by macroeconomic forces. In the decade thereafter, globalized "western" financial markets, and their rampantly self-seeking financiers, wreaked havoc on the world.

For political historian Halim Barakat (1993), in his seminal book *The Arab World*:

> *The triumph of capitalism in Eastern Europe has led many western leaders and intellectuals to prematurely declare the triumph of capitalism, while overlooking its western shortcomings. Even liberalism may no longer have a place on the world map. The mainstream has shifted from the centre to the right. What is lacking is a balance between freedom and equality. In their search for democracy, the Arabs, the great majority of whom suffer from poverty, cannot afford to accept western democracy if it excludes equality and social justice as constituent elements . . . .*

Unfortunately, overall though, the endemic tendency to fragment and to split, between "Islam and the West", or between Shia and Sunni, if not also between Israel and Palestine, has inhibited such self-determination, which for us is a fourfold rather than a singular and a polarized pursuit. So how do we go from here to there? We vigorously maintain that capitalism has neither been the beginning, nor is the end of the story, but is ripe itself (this for us is the real meaning of the recent credit crunch) for a fundamental transformation, that is, as long as we can get away from the sterile debate between twofold capitalism and socialism, or even between private enterprise and state control, the "west" and the "rest". So the substantive forces that might promote such transformation span a quaternity rather than a polarity. Such forces come first, then, from the *relational* "south", represented by *environmentalism* (nature and community); second, such forces of *renewal* come from the "east", represented by our version of *culturalism* (culture and spirituality). These, then, are to be followed, rather than preceded, by voices from the "north", represented, for example, by movements that promote *democratic socialism*, and ultimately from the "west", where *economic opportunity* beckons.

Environmentalism: towards healing the planet

Reform not transform

On countless occasions we have had conversations with "progressive" management thinkers, organization developers, or agents of change within enterprises and communities, consultancies and universities, who have advocated "transformation". Whether in the form of new forms of spiritual consciousness, new kinds of organization structure, new approaches to

Table 4.1 Integral enterprise in society

Embodying Integral Enterprise in Society: Relational Effect   *Environmentalism; culturalism; democracy; sustainability*   Heal planet; peacefully co-evolve; open society; economic opportunity
• *Attributes of Embodiment* – RELATIONAL PATH: <u>Grounding</u> – Goko personal and communal engagement; <u>Emergence</u> – calabash of group knowledge sharing; <u>Navigation</u> – GENE rhythm of social innovation; <u>Effect</u> – *integral realities/societal transformation*. RENEWAL PATH: <u>Grounding</u> – integral state; <u>Emergence</u> – institutional integration; <u>Navigation</u> – releasing GENE-ius; <u>Effect</u> – societal renaissance. REASONED REALIZATION PATH: <u>Grounding</u> – school education for all the senses; <u>Emergence</u> – enterprise learning and development; <u>Navigation</u> – sustainable development university; <u>Effecting</u> – institutional genealogy.   • *Integrator role*: **Lessem and Schieffer.**   • *GENE of integral enterprise in society*: *Grounded* in nature and community: ***community building*** functionally aligned with **environmentalism** societally; *emerging* through culture and spirituality via ***conscious evolution*** functionally aligned with **culturalism** societally; *navigating* through science and technology via ***knowledge creation*** functionally aligned with **social democracy** societally; *effected* economics and finance through ***sustainable development*** functionally aligned with overall ***sustainability*** societally, creating a world without poverty.

corporate responsibility or new varieties of communications technology, the one thing you can guarantee is that none of these approaches touches the underlying ideology, that is, capitalism and the financial markets that serve to support it. In fact, when we have challenged such a "head-in-the-sands" orientation, the conventional response has been twofold.

On the one hand, there are those who argue that capitalism is sacrosanct, and cannot be questioned, unless we are advocating, like some latter-day Don Quixote, state socialism once again. The other conventional response, perhaps like that of a Bill Gates or a Richard Branson, is that modern-day capitalism is something lamentable, and is therefore in need of reform, leading, as such, to *creative* capitalism, for Gates, and *Gaia* capitalism for Branson. Re-form not trans-form, is their progressive capitalist mantra.

The advent of environmentalism

Of late, though, *environmentalism* has been rapidly, and potentially more transformatively, coming into its own, and our Citizens' Initiative on *Integral Green Slovenia* (Piciga *et al.*, 2016; see Chapter 12 below) reflects just that. American environmentalist and social activist Paul Hawken, author of *Natural Capitalism*, in his more recent *Blessed Unrest: How the Largest Social Movement in History is Restoring Grace, Justice and Beauty* (2008) reveals how environmental activism, social justice initiatives and indigenous cultures' "southern" resistance to globalization have become intertwined, to collectively express the needs, in the new millennium, of the majority of people on Earth. In fact, Peter Senge and his colleagues, in *The Necessary Revolution: How Individuals and Organizations are Working Together to Create a Sustainable World* (2010), take the story on from there. For them the industrial age has brought extraordinary improvements in public education, human rights and material wellbeing, but it has destroyed ecosystems and swallowed up traditional cultures that have thrived for centuries, and created a way of life that cannot continue for much longer. In this sense, climate change is a particular sort of gift, a time clock telling us how fast the industrial age is ending.

That said, while such environmentalists pay a lot of attention to cultural, as well as natural, diversity, they fail to draw on the particularities of each culture, whether Southern African or Northern European, Shona or Swedish, and how such cultural specificity has, in each case, its unique contribution to make to our world. Mexico, then, is such a case in point. It is to this country we now turn.

Culturalism: towards peaceful co-evolution

Grassroots post-modernism

We continue from where Hawken and Senge and colleagues have left off, albeit now in a more "south-eastern" guise. Mexico's renowned social activist Gustavo Esteva, and Penn State's Indian-born Professor of Education Madhu Prakash (2014), view the inevitable breakdown of the industrial age, in terms that,

> *terrorize modern minorities, thereby being transformed by non-modern majorities into opportunities for regenerating their own traditions, their cultures, their unique indigenous and other non-modern arts of living and dying.*

In telling their "non-modern" stories the authors encourage these societies to learn from their communal ingenuity and cultural arts, so as to go beyond the mono-culturalism of the modern world, inspired to weave the fabric of their evolving epic: to retain and regenerate their culture, despite the odds that threaten their lives and spaces. However, in our own "culturalist" terms, it is the juxtaposition of tradition and modernity, the local and the global, the indigenous and the exogenous that is the key to peaceful co-evolution between peoples, and indeed to societal renewal. In fact, while indigenous societies in Latin American today – Bolivia, Ecuador, Peru, Venezuela – are newly asserting themselves, perhaps the best-known instance of such renewal, which is taking place through the exposure, on an enormous scale, of hitherto marginalized peoples to classical music in Venezuela, is an example of this.

Japanese spirit / Western technique

In a more techno-economic and "north-eastern" context, the Japanese miracle, in the latter part of the last century, had a "culturist" tale to tell, when the term "Japanese Spirit / Western Technique" became something of a buzzword in business circles. Why has this island nation, Japanese social philosopher Taichi Sakaiya asked then (1993), suddenly become the world's purest industrial society? Since the Meiji period Japan has acquired many technologies from Europe and America. Without this knowledge, industrialization would not have proceeded. But in the Islamic world, India and China also came into contact with European and American technologies. Why, then, did these countries not develop similarly, at least now until very recently? If contact with knowledge, technology and systems were enough, every country would be a modern industrial state. Europe underwent years of conflict between competing aesthetic and ethical systems from the Renaissance onwards before industrial civilization took root. Developers of new technologies were sometimes burnt as witches.

Japan accepted modernization more quickly than any other nation had done, in the last forty years. Japan, furthermore, has longstanding traditions that facilitate the embrace of foreign technology and systems and their digestion. Virtually all Japanese have a Shinto marriage and a Buddhist funeral. They visit Shinto shrines for the New Year's prayers and Buddhist festivals for the Festival of the Dead, while meditating in Zen temples and even perhaps celebrating Christmas. In Korea, Confucians, Buddhists and Christians intermingle, but their believers are distinct. In most countries people believe in one religion at a time. This phenomenon, then, whereby religions are fused together, is the same one that enabled the Japanese to accept Western civilization so easily. Prince Shotoku, a political genius in the seventh century, discovered a way to reconcile Buddhism, Shinto and Confucianism. He proclaimed that adding something new did not negate the old. We now turn from nature and culture to the socio-political, before ending up, rather than beginning, with economics.

Democratic socialism: towards open society

Social protection to network society

For the contemporary Eastern European philosopher based in the UK, in the 1930s, Karl Polanyi, there are two organizing principles in society (Polanyi, 2001). One is that of economic liberalism (shareholder capitalism), relying on the support of the trading classes, using free trade; the other was the principle of social protection (democratic socialism). The latter aimed at the conservation of man and nature as well as productive organization, using protective legislation, restrictive association and instruments of intervention, something that characterizes the Nordic societies today, and has been a key constituent of the Finnish economic miracle, from the 1990s onwards.

In fact, for contemporary Spanish sociologist Manuel Castells (2000), as we saw in our previous volume – note that both Polanyi and Castells are both continental European, what we term "northern" –, trade unions do not disappear in what he terms the post-modern network society. But, depending on their strategies, they might become trenches of resistance to economic and technological change, or powerful actors of innovation on the new meaning of work and wealth creation in a production system based on flexibility, autonomy and creativity. *The network society, as such, is manifested in a transformation of sociability. Internet users are more social, more socially and politically active than non-users.* Similarly, new forms of wireless, mobile and SMS communication increase sociability. People fold technology into their lives.

Toward the knowledge creating society

More often than not it happens that the necessary adaptation of the work-force to the new conditions of innovation and productivity is manipulated by companies to their advantage. For Castells, that is ultimately self-defeating, as it distances the workforce from the enterprise. Indeed, for Polanyi as for Castells, a narrow conception of self-interest, such as a liberal and positivist one, must lead to a warped world vision of social and political history. For *no purely objective and monetary definition of interests can leave room for that vital need for subjective interest and social protection.* For Nonaka and Takeuchi (1995), the process of "socialization" starts off the knowledge creating process, which thereby is an essentially communal affair. Moreover, as is clearly apparent in all societies, the state, or public sector, has a major role to play in establishing schools and universities, where knowledge is generated and disseminated. We finally turn to economic sustainability, and opportunity.

Economic opportunity: creating a world without poverty

For our ultimate, "western" and economic port of call, rather than attaching ourselves to yet another "ism" – like environmentalism, culturalism or democratic socialism – and now departing fundamentally from "capitalism", we introduce the overall concept of *Sustainability* with a difference. That difference is underlined by the overall, "southern" *relational* approach we have adopted in this chapter, on *effecting* integral development.

As such, Mfuniselwa Bhengu (2015), of Zulu African origin, an ex-South African member of parliament and writer on African philosophy, most specifically related to "cultural economics", has come up with a new economic term:

> The author is tempted to coin a new term for a sustainable economic system as "Mnothonomics". Mnotho is a Nguni word meaning economics, therefore, it is mnotho + economics = mnothonomics. In other words, the term mnotho would signify African grounding identity whilst the term economics would signify global integrity: mnothonomics.

On that "southern" original note we conclude our societal journey, which has hopefully provided you, the reader, with a first intimation of the major streams of thought serving to build up an Integral Society.

So, where does all of this lead?

Conclusion: from integral societies to an integral world

Over the past decade, around Trans4m Centre for Integral Development, we have grown into an international community of transformation agents, and transformational structures. We are dedicated to taking the story forwards, helping organizations, communities and societies to become more sustainable, by successfully addressing the burning issues today's organizations and societies are facing. We have grouped these burning issues into four main categories, again applying a Four World integral perspective:

1 *Healing the Planet*: Supplanting Communal and Environmental Decay.
2 *Peaceful Co-evolution*: Overcoming Global Domination and Local Fundamentalism.
3 *Building Open Societies*: Transcending Narrow Parochialism and Rampant Corruption.
4 *Economic Opportunity*: Creating a World without Poverty.

If you like, these four core issues are the "fourfold vision" we hold. They form the inner motif of our transformational journey, ultimately with a view to embodying integral development, in enterprise and in society. Closing with William Blake's beautiful "fourfold poem", we invite you to join us on that journey!

> *Now I a fourfold vision see,*
> *And a fourfold vision is given to me:*
> *'Tis fourfold in my supreme delight*
> *And threefold in soft Beulah's night*
> *And twofold always, may God us keep*
> *From Single Vision and Newton's sleep!*
> William Blake

We now turn from the relational to the renewal path, starting out by grounding such embodiment of integral development in the "integral state".

References

Barakat, H. (1993) *The Arab World: Society, Culture and State*. Los Angeles, CA: University of California Press
Bhengu, M. (2015) *Amazulu: Ancient Egyptian Origin – Spirit Beyond the Heavens*. Durban: Mepho Publishers.
Castells, M. (2000) *The Rise of the Network Society: Economy, Society and Culture*. Chichester: Wiley-Blackwell.

Esteva, E. and Prakash, M. (2014) *Grassroots Post-Modernism: Remaking the Soil of Cultures. 2nd edition*. London: Zed Books.

Hawken, P. (2008) *Blessed Unrest: How the Largest Social Movement in History is restoring Grace, Justice and Beauty*. New York: Penguin Books.

Lessem, R. and Schieffer, A. (2009) *Transformation Management: Toward the Integral Enterprise*. Abingdon: Routledge.

Lessem, R., Abouleish, I., Pogacnik, M. and Herman, L. (2014) *Integral Polity: Aligning Nature, Culture, Society and Economy*. Abingdon: Routledge.

Nonaka, I. and Takeuchi, H. (1995) *The Knowledge Creating Company*. Oxford: Oxford University Press.

Perlas, N. (2003) *Shaping Globalisation: Civil Society, Cultural Power and Threefolding*. Vancouver, BC: New Society Publishers.

Piciga, D., Schieffer, A. and Lessem, R. (2016) *Integral Green Slovenia: Towards a Social Knowledge and Value Based Society and Economy at the Heart of Europe*. Abingdon: Routledge.

Polanyi, K. (2001) *The Great Transformation: The Political and Economic Origins of our Time. 2nd Edition*. New York: Beacon Press.

Sakaiya, T. (1993) *What is Japan? Contradictions and Transformations*. Tokyo: Kodansha.

Senge, P. *et al.* (2010) *The Necessary Revolution: How Individuals and Organizations are Working Together to Create a Sustainable World*. New York: Nicolas Brealey.

Steiner, R. (1977) *Towards Social Renewal*. Forest Row, East Sussex: Rudolf Steiner Publishers.

Part II

Renewal path

Awaken consciousness to institutional research

5 Grounding

The integral state

Summary of chapter:

1 a grounded commonwealth entails the association and spirit of public belonging;
2 an emergent regime secures acceptance and legitimacy in wider society;
3 a competent administration provides reliable, trustworthy public institutions;
4 able leadership embodies a potentially and ultimately integral state effect.

Introduction: renewal path to grounding embodied development

Stated forms and frames

So far we have focused on the relational path, embodying integral development, personally and communally, organizationally and societally, through grounding and emergence, navigating and effecting development, respectively. We now turn more concertedly towards the path of renewal, with a view to integral embodiment, starting with in this case societal grounding.

In introducing as such our journey towards an "*integral* state", or indeed polity (Lessem *et al.*, 2014), we begin in an unlikely place, that is, in Somalia, albeit from the perspective of Somalian-born but American-bred political scientists Abdi and Ahmed Samatar (2002), founders of the Institute for Global Citizenship at Macalester College, in the US Twin States. On the African ground to begin with, then, we recognize a full continuum, between – for them – the *forms* of the "cadaverous" state at one negative extreme, and their positive "integral" expression, at the other. Prior to this, moreover, we shall consider the different political *frames*,

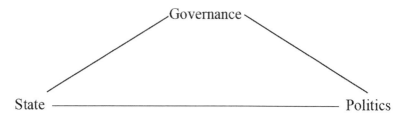

Figure 5.1 Governance, state and politics

which resonate with our own progressive release of GENE-ius, as we shall see. Moreover, and from the outset, we have selected a Muslim country, Somalia in this case, because without finding an integral orientation to an Islamic political future (see the case of Oman in that respect, Chapter 8), the world at large, or international polity, has little hope of realizing itself in fully functional guise.

For Ahmed Samatar and his brother Abdi, then, basic or primal political activities precede the appearance of the state. Such primordial groups, typified by small bands and by intimacy or, more precisely, kin attachments, have existed and continue to survive, ever so precariously in Somalia or as the Bushmen in the Kalahari Desert of Botswana, without a formal authority structure solely designed to perform political tasks.

Such communities negotiate myriad individual and family interests and idiosyncrasies, in addition to the vagaries of the general material and cultural context, through custom and a set of reciprocal but not necessarily equal arrangements. These early aggregations of large, but by no means universal, interests and networks, provision of public goods, and the subsequent investments of authority in persons embedded in such institutions, for the Samatars, give glimpses of some of the enduring characteristics of what we contemporaneously identify as the state.

Governance, states and politics

The evolution of the idea and structuring of the state, then, is complicated, for the Samatars, and has numerous variations. What is relevant here is to note its ancient pedigree, define its morphology, and point towards its key attributes. They define the state, as such, as

> *a constellation of norms, and institutions including those who inhabit them, ostensibly to manage the collective political fate of a given society.*

+   -

Integral   *Developmental*   *Predental*   *Predatory*   *Cadaverous*

Figure 5.2 Forms of state

Political destiny includes significant contradictions and concerns that add up to such political identity and direction. Structurally, a state, for the Samatars, has the following features: *monopoly on coercion, specific territorial boundaries, a relatively fixed population, economic and cultural functions, sovereignty, and recognition by other states and their organizations.* This supreme public power, that is, the state, is "a historical phenomenon" – a creation of human beings in interaction, which, in turn, also acts in profound ways upon individual and collective life.

The Samatars then start with political *Frames*, which we shall now relate to our own integral approach to releasing GENE-ius, here in a political context.

Frames of state: commonwealth to leadership

Grounding to effect

The state, then, is not some formless thing. Rather, its internal constitution can be anatomized. The Samatars suggest, heuristically, four main elements that make up the state: a commonwealth, a regime, an administration and a leader. For us,

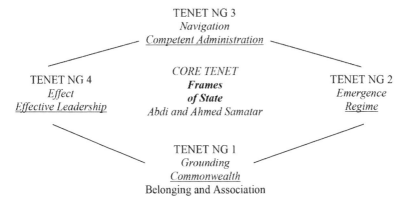

Figure 5.3 Renewal frames of state: grounding tenets

- the commonwealth provides the underlying *grounding*;
- a regime promotes *emergence*;
- a competent administration underlies *navigation*; and
- able leadership embodies a potentially and ultimately integral *effect*.

We now consider each in turn.

Grounded in an original commonwealth

The primal element of the state is the foundational commonwealth. In its most inclusive sense, this *entails the association and spirit of public belonging* that is not easily derailed by narrow impulses. In fact, we see it described in our "southern" grounding as set out in volume 3 of the CARE-ing for Integral Development series, *Innovation Driven Institutional Research*, by Chancellor Williams, in his "original democracy" *constituting Africa.*

To create an identity large enough to accommodate kinship with the other, naturally and communally, beyond filial or other exclusive affiliations, is to transmute self into citizen – the oldest of the challenges, for the Samatars, to the establishment of a political community. Here, then, *individual or group interest engages the imperative of a natural and communal bond* characterized in the felicitous expression of Ireland's nineteenth-century political

Table 5.1 Reasoned realization of frames of state

Embodying Integral Development: Grounding State Reason *Frames of state: towards the integral state* Associative commonwealth to effective leadership
• *Attributes of Embodiment* – RELATIONAL PATH: Grounding – Goko personal and communal engagement; Emergence – calabash of group knowledge sharing; Navigation – GENE rhythm of social innovation; Effect – integral realities/societal transformation. RENEWAL PATH: Grounding – *integral state*; Emergence – institutional integration; Navigation – releasing GENE-ius; Effect – societal renaissance. REASONED REALIZATION PATH: Grounding – school education for all the senses; Emergence – enterprise learning and development; Navigation – sustainable development university; Effecting – institutional genealogy. • *Integrator role*: embodied leader, e.g. ***Abdi and Ahmed Samatar***. • *Societal development GENE: grounded* in a ***commonwealth*** promoting a sense of belonging and association; *emerging* through a ***regime*** that secures acceptance and legitimacy in the wider society; *navigating* through ***a competent administration*** underscoring the infrastructure of the state, that is, reliable and trustworthy public institutions; finally the ***effective leader*** immediately and ultimately embodies the state in question.

philosopher, Edmund Burke: "common affections". In fact, and for many in Britain ironically, the chief philosophical champion of what has come to be termed the "Big Society" movement, Philip Blond (2010), has been attempting to bring Burke's communal–political orientation back into British public favour, so as to counteract the predominating individualism that is causing no end of societal problems, with more of a sense of an original, and resurrected, *Commonwealth*. Thereafter follows what they term a legitimate political "regime".

An emergent regime as political foundation

Returning then to the Samatars, an emergent <u>regime</u>, such as a council of elders, *is a constellation of officials assigned to the highest portfolios of executive authority*. If a regime is to attain any modicum of acceptance and legitimacy by the larger society, self or factional gain would have to be tamed by a combination of inclusive aspiration, a consciousness of needs, ethical and legal conduct, and effective management. This would invariably involve marrying up elements of tradition, and modernity, in a particular context.

Thus, *members of a successful regime are the custodians of a community or society's ideals, of the beliefs it cherishes, of its permanent hopes, of the faith that makes a nation out of a mere aggregation of individuals.* The regime cannot limit itself solely to the role of the keeper of tradition and noble ambition; rather, progress depends on the intellect to detect and the courage to articulate the hidden, and even the unutterable, elements of what is often called "vision." Such a vision would indeed combine the indigenous with the exogenous. The Samatars then turn to competent administration.

Competent administration as navigation-and-emancipation

The <u>administrative</u> *frame underscores the infrastructure of the state.* Here are located *institutions* (e.g. civil service, courts, law enforcement, and educational policy, facilities, curricula and personnel) *that carry out the day-to-day assignments and preserve procedures and documents of the operations of the state.* This is important for the way a society governs itself – one that presents a test case for a regime to monitor itself, the relative autonomy of offices and institutions, and their competence. Without such a rationally based administration, building on what has come before, there can be no thoroughgoing emancipation. However, if such administration is simply, and bureaucratically, imposed from above, repression will replace emancipation.

In other words, the greater the compliance with authentically derived rules and regulations, that is, those which serve to balance out tradition and modernity, the larger the dividends for both a regime's reputation and the viability of public life and order. In contrast, the more the operational organs are tied to the whims of a parochial, self-serving, regime interest, the greater the degree of evaporation of the rightfulness of all three frames. This is the ultimate cost of incompetence and corruption, whereby significant and inescapable alienation comes with the momentary victory of one group.

Authentic, and would-be integral administration, by contrast, absorbs the divisive fallout from oppositional politics. The result is the return of the state, through sound governance, to societal ownership, a source of competence and an architect of common destiny. *Without a prior grounding of a spirit of belonging, and a prior regime able to build on this, excessive particularity becomes the norm – the antithesis of a national project.* Nepotism and bureaucratic administration, through the operations of the state, then, is an unavoidable and contradictory activity that at once unveils centrifugal issues and facilitates centripetal ideas and action.

In weighing the balance of the tension between difference and commonality, it is the latter, albeit accommodating the former, that defines the health of political life in a given society. For, beyond the struggle for power, a rather narrow objective that could easily lead to a desolation of the spirit, *a polity fit for "symbiotic creatures" is the art of associating men [and women] for the purpose of establishing, cultivating, and conserving social life among them.* Finally, the Samatars turn to "able leadership".

Effective able leadership and beyond

We turn finally to effective leadership. *The* effective <u>leader</u>, then, in the final analysis, and like a Nelson Mandela in the best possible sense, duly revisiting his or her commonwealth of origin, *is the individual who immediately and ultimately embodies the state in question.* He/ she can make a positive difference in his/her time, leaving behind a legacy of competence, constitutionalism and order. However, the leader can also preside over ineptness, corruption and institutional disarray, whose consequences include an undermining of constructive efforts by others and the killing of civic spirit. He or she then needs to build on the spirited commonwealth, the regime constellation and the competent administration that comes before (see the next chapter), thereby for us becoming something of an integrator.

We now turn from frames to *forms* of state, and at that point we introduce – via the noted Italian political philosopher of the previous century, Antonio Gramsci (2000) – the notion of the *integral* state, or polity.

Forms of state

Integral to cadaverous

Each of the four frames of the state, much like the parts of a body, performs at once its own local functions and works in concert with the rest to keep the whole purring along. Any damage to one means trouble for the others; and when the accumulation of deficiencies becomes greater than the assets, the state and its society are confronted with major problems. Put more precisely, in addition to the vitality of the frames, the degree of health or morbidity of the state is also conditioned by its history, endowments of its society, including its nature and its culture, and the vagaries of regional and transnational circumstances.

Such a configuration of frames and forces produces different state forms that, in descending order from positive to negative, and in turn, have consequences for the seminal project of development. States, for the Samatars, come in many guises (see Figure 5.3) above. For the sake of parsimony, however, one could offer a spectrum that registers five possible types that vary from, at one extreme, the highly effective – integral – to its opposite, the dead – cadaverous. The primary distinguishing factors include (a) the wholeness of each frame; (b) the degree of coordination; and (c) the depth of interior attachments to fellowship and collective realization.

Integral state: delicately balanced

Since no state is immune to the vicissitudes that result from the jostling among individuals as well as larger social forces, a quintessential element of human historicity, an <u>integral state,</u> is, for Gramsci as for the Samatars, *emblematic of a moment of delicate balance*, serving to build up a mentality of collective stake-holding and exude hope. Gramsci's integral state, then, does not only succeed in delivering public goods but, particularly important, the leadership generates a degree of moral and intellectual bonding with the citizens. This "organic" affiliation is central to the establishment of the "national–popular". Africa as such, for the Samatars, has yet to produce an integral state.

Developmental state: positively proactive

If such a state, then, is the guardian of an integral polity and general prosperity, a <u>developmental state</u> is the next best project. In this context, the state is *conspicuously activist in both the improvement of human capital and the enhancement of the productive forces and national accumulation*. But, as has often been the case, achievements in the economic and social realms may come at the cost of civic pluralism and basic liberties. Specifically, nature and culture may suffer at the hands of society and economy. Because the developmental state is primarily driven by ambition to quickly mollify external and domestic vulnerabilities of the society, such a singular attention leaves little room for open dissent and debate.

In the end, a developmental state is visibly Janus faced – impressive in marshalling resources and building economic capacity, but relatively less attentive to the creation of an ambience conducive to republican individuation. Moreover, and in acute cases, heavy disincentives are presented to those who dare to disagree or insist on moral autonomy. There are exceptions to the discrepancy between development and democracy, as the case of Botswana demonstrates. The Botswana state has been Africa's premier developmental state. Despite the shackles inherited from British colonialism, the state has qualitatively transformed its society from a South African labour reserve to one of the fastest-growing economies in the world for the better part of the last thirty-five years. Botswana has maintained genuine commitment to liberal democracy since independence. This blending of development and democracy makes Botswana unique among developmental states. Botswana has some of the ingredients, most specifically political and economic, necessary for establishing an integral state.

Prebendal state: self-protective

Next in descending order, a <u>prebendal</u> state is typically *preoccupied with the protection and reproduction of the immediate interests of a regime and its associates*. At the same time, the economy becomes a source of personal and group enrichment, usually in the form of shady rent seeking, and the political institutions amount to little more than a haven for personal privilege. A key feature of a prebendal state is high dependency – a combination of subservience to external powers, venality, and despotism at home. Unless turned around, and there is time and space for such action, these liabilities increasingly blunt any developmental propulsion, creating a general culture of disregard for the common good.

Nigeria, historically for the Samatars, has been the archetypical prebendal state, though in recent years, in the new millennium, there have been moves afoot to evolve in a developmental, if not even integral, direction (Gramsci, 2000). In fact, it even degenerated into a predatory institution under successive civilian and military regimes. The cost of predation became exceedingly onerous under General Abacha's regime. Consequently, key organs of civil society struggled against the regime during much of the 1990s.

At the end, the military retreated and a civilian government was elected. Retired General Obasanjo's leadership of the past decade made some encouraging attempts in rebuilding public institutions so they may gain legitimacy and sufficient capacity to meet the development needs of the Nigerian society. Nonetheless, heavy reliance on rent from oil, ethnic and religious antagonism, and a misappropriation of national wealth continue to be part of political practice, which some members of Trans4m's doctoral research community, under the guise of CISER (Centre for Social and Economic Research) and ACIRD (African Centre for Integral Research and Development) – see previous volume, *Innovation Driven Institutional Research* – are seeking to redress (Oshodi, 2014).

Predatory state: diabolical politics

Penultimately the predatory state is *synonymous with diabolical politics*. When the prebendal state loses what little functional capacity and stability it had, alienation mounts apace. No more even a symbol of disordered legitimacy, the last veils of collective belonging drop, and scavenging over dwindling public resources becomes openly vicious. For the regime, with an ever-narrowing grid, leadership turns into its antithesis – that is, cruel selfishness that slides into open criminality. In the meantime, as decay advances, a mixture of shock and hyper-anxiety over personal and family survival becomes the paradigm of social and political conduct. With the full atrophy of the vital functions of the state, the centaurs become one-dimensional beasts.

Together, these factors dissipate the stock of citizenship and mark the beginnings of the death of civic virtue. In fact, without development of the material and intellectual productive forces, any society risks becoming gradually and unwittingly stagnant and turning in on itself, becoming less able to cope with the effects of internal conflicts. Mobutu's Zaire, and Taylor's Liberia, for the Samatars, come to mind as proximate examples.

Cadaverous state: degenerative polity

Sadly and finally, the predatory state may not be the last stop in the glide towards optimum degeneration; it can get worse – the cadaverous state. With heightened physical and economic insecurity, and the evaporation of public discourse and life, many take flight to anywhere before the final curtain. Those who stay behind are enveloped by a new barbarism, one defined by a looting of what is left of the commons, further retailing of identities, and prodigality of terror. Thus spoke Nigeria literary giant Wole Soyinka (1997), as he reflected on such happenings in parts of the continent:

How does a sculptor begin to carve with only stumps for arms? How does a village griot ply his trade with only the root of the tongue still lodged at the gateway of memory? The rest has been cut out—often the hand that wields the knife is the hand of the future, the ubiquitous child-soldier—and the air is bereft even of the solace of its lament. A lament can be purifying, consoling, for a lament still affirms the retention of soul, even of faith, yes, it is a cry of loss, of bereavement, an echo of pain but is, therefore, an affirmation of humanity, a reaching out to the world that is still human or to forces that shape humanity.

A lament does not emerge from atrocities, for an atrocity is the very silencing of the human voice. It deadens the soul and clogs up the passages of hope, opening up in their place only sterile accusa-tions, the resolve of vengeance, or else a total surrender to the tri-umph of banality. We can no longer speak of wars on the continent, only arenas of competitive atrocities.

The end point of such an experience is the cadaverous state. Every frame is damaged to such an extreme extent that civic life is, simply put, no more. An immediate lesson is how easy it is to demolish in quick time what has taken years to build. The Somali case is an instantiation of this type. So where, for the Samatars, does an Islamic society (not *Islamist*) like Somalia go from here?

Conclusion: reasoned options of governance

Democratic and developmental stance

To the extent that the Samatars' home country Somalia, for them in the new millennium, then, has become such a cadaverous state, where might it go from here, in embodying integral, societal development? Such a devel-opmental, or even ultimately integral, scenario, would integrate the best of Somali kinship, Islamic piety, and democracy and development. The Somali tradition of kinship (as distinct from clanism and beset with male dominance) emphasizes general fairness, generosity, and obedience to God.

At the heart of a worldly Islamic philosophy, for the Samatars, is the promotion of peace, justice, and equality for all. "The basic élan of the Quran," writes Fazhur Rahman (2009), is its "stress on socioeconomic justice and essential egalitarianism." Democracy's chief characteristics include individual liberty, choice and constitutional accountability of power, while development underscores a perpetual but measured transfor-mation of the cultural, environmental, scientific, economic and political spheres of the society.

Essential indices for gauging such a strategy are an accent on ethical competence and legitimate achievement; tolerance, if not respect for, nuance and diversity through a normalization of *Ijtihad*, that is, advancement or even transformation; and freedom of thinking in a non-coercive atmosphere. No Muslim country in the modern world has fully achieved this scenario. For the Samatars, a few are slowly moving in that direction, however, such as Turkey and Malaysia. Together, transition and synthesis are tantamount to a gearing up for a new ontology. That assignment and what is at stake are even more apparent today.

The struggle for Islamic cosmopolitanism

If Somalis make headway in their epochal project, for the Samatars, then, they will have added a precious contribution to the struggle for an *Islamic cosmopolitan-ism* robust enough to co-exist comfortably with the multicivilizational modern world and to negotiate successfully the ambiguities of globalization. To be sure, this is the most daunting option – one whose pursuit will require all the intelligence, creativity, dexterity, discipline and patience that Somalis can muster. Despite the enormous difficulties, it is a journey pleasing to Allah, possible and most thrilling to begin against the humiliating political squalor of the present.

Somalis, for the Samatars in conclusion, are no different from other societies in that none could meet its basic collective needs (ranging from security to environmental and economic wellbeing to education and scientific advancement) without an effective public power. As Adam Smith, the great sage of the Scottish Enlightenment, taught us centuries ago, "the authority and security of civil government is a necessary condition for the flourishing of liberty, reason, and happiness of humankind" ([1776] 2003).

While this is uniform across the modern world, the imperative is greatest among late-developing societies. The state is not and cannot be everything, but its absence is a form of acute social homelessness. Even the World Bank, contemporary apostle of market economics, made this landmark assertion in 1997, with regard to the indispensability of the state for a viable society:

> Good government is not a luxury, it is a vital necessity for development . . . an effective state is vital for the provision of goods and service, and the rules and institutions that allow markets to flourish, people to lead healthier, happier lives.

The condition of the past sixteen years testifies to the supreme deficits that come with the destruction of national political structures. Another decade or more of the present situation is too horrible to contemplate. But, in order to construct a new national and effective state, Somalis will have to address this most difficult of issues: the resurrection of a vibrant people-hood. More generally, then, and in terms of embodying integral development, at a state level, duly grounded in the path of reasoned realization: *a grounded commonwealth entails the association and spirit of public belonging; an emergent regime that secures acceptance and legitimacy in wider society; a competent administration providing reliable, trustworthy public institutions; able leadership embodies a potentially and ultimately integral state effect.*

We now turn from grounding to emergence, on the path of renewal, with a view to embodying integral development, now individually and organizationally.

References

Blond, P. (2010) *Red Tory: How Left and Right have Broken Britain and How We Can Fix It*. London: Bloomsbury.

Gramsci, A. (2000) *A Gramsci Reader*. London. Lawrence & Wishart.

Lessem, R., Abouleish, I., Pocagnik, M. and Herman, L. (2014) *Integral Polity: Aligning Nature, Culture, Society and Economy*. Abingdon: Routledge.

Oshodi, B. (2014) *An Integral Approach to Development Economics: Islamic Finance in an African Context*. Farnham: Gower.

Rahman, F. (2009) *Major Themes of the Qur'an: Second Edition*. Chicago, IL: Chicago University Press.

Samatar, Abdi and Samatar, Ahmed, eds (2002) *The African State: Reconsiderations*. Portsmouth, NH: Heinemann.

Soyinka, W. (1997) *The Open Sore of the Continent: Personal Narrative on the Nigerian Crisis*. Oxford: Oxford University Press.

6 Emerging
Institutional integration

Summary of chapter:

1   individual evolving in stages – entrepreneur, manager, leader, to integrator;
2   organization evolving in stages – pioneering, differentiation, integration;
3   becoming an integrated organization;
4   effect transformation – transcendent commonwealth/organizational ecosystem.

Introduction: a need to evolve

Leadership frustration

This second emergent chapter, in renewing integral embodiment, focuses on the evolution of enterprise and entrepreneurship, towards management, leadership and thereafter integration, in theory if not altogether in practice. In fact we take on from where the Samatars have left off, with their focus on able, in their case political, leadership, arguing here, however, in our ultimate focus on *Integrators* (Lessem, 2016), that we need to go *Beyond Leadership*.

While such focus may be seen as a long way from the integral state, this chapter is born out of a particular, personal frustration, on the one hand, and a great opportunity, on the other. And the two are connected. First comes the frustration. As a student, teacher and practitioner of, and consultant in, business management over the last fifty years, in America (Harvard Business School in Cambridge), Britain (City University Business School in London), continental Europe (Institute of Management Development, IMD, in Lausanne, Switzerland) and South Africa (Wits Graduate Business School in Johannesburg) as well as Zimbabwe (Zimbabwe University Business School in Harare), I am enormously frustrated by the recent eclipse of the management of organizations, in favour of individual leadership. In fact, by analogy with the Samatars, it is as if we needed able leaders, while lacking competent administration, not to mention the underlying commonwealth-and-community that need to come before, and the integral state thereafter. In the same way, then, as we need an emergent innovation ecosystem, arising out of an integral consciousness, so we also need an "integrator ecosystem".

Having been immersed for decades in the inordinate richness of management *and organizational* literature, spanning not only all the variegated business functions but also the development of self, organization and society, I find the excessive focus on *individual* leadership today, bereft of the management of organizations, to be incredibly myopic. In fact, as the Dean of Harvard College, Professor Rakesh Khurana has put it, in his *Higher Aims to Hired Hands* (2007):

> *Eventually business schools began responding to the clarion call for developing leaders, not managers. In the 1990's, for example, Harvard shifted from its emphasis on general management to "educating leaders who make a difference in the world". One of the central features of a bone fide profession is a coherent body of expert knowledge built upon a well-developed theoretical foundation. The renowned American business executive and writer Chester Barnard in fact observed in the 1930's that the "Great Man" view on leadership generated "an extraordinary amount of dogmatically stated nonsense". Leadership, as such, lacks a usable body of knowledge to go with it.*

And times have not changed! Interestingly enough, leadership can represent some kind of evolution from pioneering entrepreneurship and "differentiated" management, so to speak. Yet this is only so if the individual leaders are eco-systemically aligned with an evolving form of "integrated" organization, in fact not unlike, polity wise, an "integral state". I ultimately call such individuals, duly aligned with their organizations *and* most especially their societies, not entrepreneurs, nor managers, nor even leaders, but organizational and societal *integrators*, each one moreover personally and culturally distinctive.

Fellow integrators' opportunity

The opportunity that has arisen, for me especially over the course of the past two decades, more recently together with my Trans4m (www.trans-4-m.com) partner Alexander Schieffer, is that we have had the good fortune, in most cases in person and in some cases in spirit, to work closely with some extraordinary integrators – together with their integrated organizations – from Africa, Europe and Asia, albeit all influenced by America.

Integrator and integration

Entrepreneur to integrator

Overall then, as such, and building on our developmental work that has come before (Schieffer and Lessem, 2014a), *personal* <u>origination</u>, for one character or another, in one place/society or another, is followed by managerial and *organizational* <u>foundation</u>. Thereafter, *individual* leadership has its subsequently <u>emancipatory</u> place, only when set within a developing self, and organization as well as a particular *society*. Finally and ultimately for us, *integral* <u>transformation</u> follows when all the above is not only differentiated but also integrated: self, organization and society, set within a particular world, in relation to other worlds, psychologically and culturally.

As such, duly aligned with an integral state, economy and enterprise, we give rise to the new notion of the "Integrator" in the twenty-first century. Such an integrator, in the second decade of the new millennium, emerges as a further evolution of personal entrepreneurship (or "intrapreneurship") in the nineteenth century, management in the mid-twentieth and leadership in the early twenty-first. Moreover, such an *integrator*, in each particular part of the world, only becomes fully such, by virtue of this differentiation and *integration*, to the extent that he or she gives rise to a newly evolved form of enterprise. Such an entity, in most cases transcending the corporate or organizational form as we know it today, has in fact already been anticipated in theory, as we shall see, but not yet, overall, been realized in practice, within particular societies. So the conventional business enterprise, and corporate institution, continue to rule the roost, around the world, whether it is appropriate or not, whether either is "pioneered", "managed" or "led". To

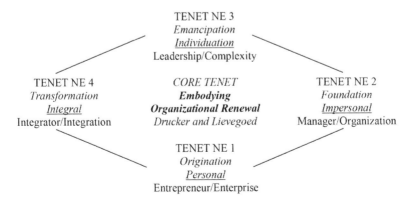

Figure 6.1 Embodying organizational renewal: emerging tenets

that extent, for example, as great as a Nelson Mandela may have been, as an individual leader, the new South Africa was bound to falter, without an integral state, and constituent integrated organizations, to match.

Such differentiation and ultimately *integration* that we are seeking, then, arises out of both a personal *individuation*, that is, self-actualization, and of societal *acculturation*, or organizational-and-cultural, thereby societal, evolution.

The evolution of enterprise

The late and great American management guru Peter Drucker, who almost singlehandedly invented the discipline of management in the first half of the last century, made the following critical point in his *Management: Tasks, Analysis and Practices* (1977):

> *The change from a business which the owner–entrepreneur can run with "helpers" to a business that requires managers, is a sweeping change. It can be made only if basic concepts, basic principles, and individual vision are changed radically. You can compare two such different kinds of business to different kinds of organism: the insect, which is held together by a tough, hard skin, and the vertebrate animal, which has a skeleton. Land animals which are supported by a hard skin cannot grow beyond a few inches in size. To be larger animals must have a skeleton. Yet the skeleton has not evolved out of the hard skin of an insect; for it is a different organ with different antecedents.*

So, from our point of view, rather than face up to the limitations of depersonalized "skeletal management", in Drucker's terms, the "leadership" fad of late has simplistically "gone back to the insect", that is, the personalized entrepreneur or leader so to speak, for a new lease of life. The only difference now, in the new millennium, is that such an "insect", as it were, as an entrepreneur on the one hand, can be *social* as well as business oriented, and a leader, on the other hand, can be *transformative* as well as transactional. So, today, you can have any kind of person at the helm of a social or economic, public or civic enterprise, as long as he or she is an "entrepreneur" or more especially now a "leader", whatever society they are in. The fact that there can be much more to leadership (we are not throwing out the leading baby with the integrating bathwater!), if it is aligned with an evolved form of organization-and-society, has passed most people by. For we like to keep things simple, and we are also creatures of habit!

What then gets left out of account, at least in our view, as for that of Harvard-based Khurana (see above) amounts to three things. *First*, an

Table 6.1 The evolution of enterprise and leadership

Embodying Integral Development: Emerging Beyond Leadership *The integrators* Commonwealth integrator to eco-integrator

- *Attributes of embodiment* – RELATIONAL PATH: <u>Grounding</u> – Goko personal and communal engagement; <u>Emergence</u> – calabash of group knowledge sharing; <u>Navigation</u> – GENE rhythm of social innovation; <u>Effect</u> – integral realities/societal transformation. RENEWAL PATH: <u>Grounding</u> – integral state; <u>Emergence</u> – *institutional integration*; <u>Navigation</u> – releasing GENE-ius; <u>Effect</u> – societal renaissance. REASONED REALIZATION PATH: <u>Grounding</u> – school education for all the senses; <u>Emergence</u> – enterprise learning and development; <u>Navigation</u> – sustainable development university; <u>Effecting</u> – institutional genealogy.
- *Integrator role*: Embodied leader, e.g. **Ahmed and Abdi Samatar**.
- *Societal development GENE*: *Grounded origination* in enterprise and personalized **entrepreneurship**; *emergent foundation* through organization and depersonalized **management**; *emancipatory navigation* through complex systems and individuating **leadership**; *effecting transformation* via integration through transcendent commonwealth to eco-**integrators**.

entrepreneur, and enterprise, should befit one kind of distinctive person, and indeed culture, or another. That is why I came up with the term *Intrapreneurs* (Lessem, 1987), to reflect such a *variegated spectrum* of initiative takers, from innovator to adventurer, as opposed to one singular type of "entrepreneur", with many such "intrapreneurs" in between, as well as the kind of variegated *Quality* organization (Lessem, 1991) to go with each. *Second*, such pioneering *enterprise*, subsequently differentiated *management* and organization (see Lievegoed's "Developing Organization" below), followed by would-be integrated *leadership* and organization – should follow each other developmentally, *each inclusive of what has come before.*

Moreover, most significantly, ultimate integration, and the integrator to go with it, transcends the very notion of an enterprise (entrepreneur), organization (management) or indeed leader (and the equivalent new "organization" form).

Developmental management and the developing organization

In the 1970s and 1980s, in fact, a new breed of business academic emerged, with a view to taking management theory, and practice, onto a next level of its evolution, leadership at that point not having assumed its current-day dominance. Pre-eminent among these thinkers, for us, was Hollander Bernard Lievegoed, who, in *The Developing Organisation* (1990), argued that the next phase in an organization's evolution, from pioneering (entrepreneurship or our intrapreneurship) and differentiation (scientific management) was that of Integration. In this phase, for him, it was crucial that the organization develop a social (unfortunately he did not distinguish between different forms of "social" and cultural – be they in our case for example English or Palestinian, Nigerian or Sri Lankan) sub-system and integrate it with the already-existing economic and technical sub-systems. For Lievegoed this is a gradual process, but an essential one. The ultimately integrated organization is characterized by the following:

- *Interlinked, smaller, relatively independent units are set up.*
- *Self-planning, self-organization and self-control ensue.*
- *It rests on the conviction that every person can and wants to develop.*
- *Personal fulfilment can be achieved in the work situation.*

Sadly, Lievegoed's *integrated* words of organizational wisdom, also aligned with *individuation*, were thereafter eclipsed by an *individualized–personalized* approach to leadership. Yet his developmental approach was by no means a voice in the wilderness. In fact, in the 1980s and 1990s, I co-evolved with the UK publisher Blackwell's a whole series of books on what we then termed *Developmental Management*, involving the work of seminal theorists, spread across diverse cultures across the globe, with whom I had become personally associated, through our mutual academic and developmental circles.

Included in this, together with Lievegoed's *European* Developing Organization, were *American*s Beck and Cowan, whose *Spiral Dynamics* (1996), introduced the notion of variegated "cultural memes", from first-tier "survival" to second-tier "integral" as well as a "Spiral Wizard" (not just a "leader") who masterminded these. *South African* Albert Koopman, through his *Transcultural Management* (1991) claimed that the object of his South African Cashbuild was "to profit a society, not merely to make a profit", thereby releasing "the divine will of Africa". He then duly practised what he preached, as a building supplies retailer, and as a cooperative association. *Canadian* Elliott Jaques, meanwhile, through his *Requisite Organization* coupled with "Executive Leadership" (1997), introduced his seven stratified layers of progressively more complex organization. Meanwhile our Indian colleague Jagdish Parikh, reflecting the "eastern" *Indian* turn in management thinking, from the 1960s to the 1990s, wrote about his life's work as a management developer in *Managing the Self: Management by Detached Involvement* (1996), which took IMD in Lausanne, Switzerland by storm.

This so-called "Developmental Management" movement was further supplemented by the work of *American* writers Peters and Waterman, famed for journey *In Search of Excellence* (1982), and thereafter we heard from the remarkable management consultant James Moore in his *The Death of Competition: Leadership and Strategy in the Age of Business Ecosystems* (1996). The notable Peter Senge was another American pioneer through his *Fifth Discipline: The Art and Practice of the Learning Organization* ([1995] 2006), followed by the seminal *Japanese* work *The Knowledge Creating Company* by Nonaka and Takeuchi (1995). Finally, even more eco-systemic in tone was Peter Block's work *Stewardship* (1993), Paul Hawken's *Natural Capitalism: The Next Industrial Revolution* ([1999] 2005) and Otto Scharmer's focus in *Leading from the Emerging Future: From Ego-system to Eco-system Economies* (Scharmer and Kaufer, 2013). What is critical for us to note is that, while writers like Senge and Scharmer explicitly included leadership in their work, *their overarching frame of reference was organizationally systemic (Senge), and societally ecosystemic (Scharmer), rather than personalized, and individualized.*

My own work at the time, in the 1980s and early 1990s, was based on *Spectral Theory* drawn from the seminal approach of British psychologist and social innovator Kevin Kingsland (see CARE volume 2, *Awakening Integral Consciousness*). Such work of mine was first embodied in so-called *Intrapreneurship*, as mentioned above, which represented my variegated individual and cultural takes on the singular notion of entrepreneurship. Subsequently, then, my Indian colleague Sudhanshu Palsule and I wrote *Managing in Four Worlds* (1997); this was followed by my more academically based *Management Development through Cultural Diversity* (1998), combining the spectral and the integral (see below). Through this work I turned from a variegated spectrum of intrapreneurs to what I then considered to be more evolved managers, organizations and leadership.

In the new millennium, moreover, with the birth of our Trans4m Centre for Integral Development in Geneva, together with Alexander Schieffer, our *integral worlds* came into being, applied to integral enterprise (Lessem, 1998), economics, (Lessem and Schieffer, 2009), research (Lessem and Schieffer, 2010a), development (Lessem and Schieffer, 2010b) and renewal (Lessem with Schieffer, 2015), among other things. Overall, as such, we brought together integral *realities* (south and east, north and west); *realms* (nature, culture, technology and economy), most especially for our purposes here integral *rhythm* (origination, foundation, emancipation and transformation), and finally integral *rounds* of self, organization, society and ultimately uni-versity.

What was missing until then, in individual person, was the notion of an *integrator* (see commonwealth to civic integrators below), serving to align the spectral and the integral, individually and institutionally, via thereby *integration*, in a particular part of the world, in specific relation to other worlds. Such a variegated integrator (integration) is both inclusive and a further accumulative evolution of the intrapreneur (enterprise), the manager (organization) and the leader (ecosystem).

Conclusion: spectral origination – the opening journey

In the final analysis, while the evolution from enterprise to management was clear cut, at least in its singular American context, the subsequent evolution of leadership, individually, was not matched, in practice, by a similarly coherent development of self-organization–society, ecosystemically. This is a matter we have here sought to address, duly following our integral rhythm (Schieffer and Lessem, 2014b), from origination (entrepreneur) to foundation (manager), on to emancipation (leader) and ultimate transformation (fully fledged integrator), critically together with the organizational counterparts of each one. We then undertake such rhythm for each of eight individually and culturally differentiated kinds of integrator, and integration, specifically involving: *grounded origination in enterprise and personalized entrepreneurship; emergent foundation through organization and depersonalized management; emancipatory navigation via complex systems and individuating leadership; effect transformation via integration – transcendent commonwealth to eco-integrators.*

The end result of such a spectral and integral journey is a cast of integrators, individually, and integration, *institutionally*, portrayed below, as Egyptian and Basque, Palestinian and Nigerian, South Africa and Sri Lankan, Anglo-American and Anglo-Indian, respectively :

*   Innovator Abouleish: Commonwealth Integrator – Sustainable *Commonwealth*; and
*   Enabler Arizemendi: Cooperative Integrator – Cooperative *Association*.

*   Executive Saayoun: Institutional Integrator – Integrated *Organization*; and
*   Animateur Adodo: Communal Integrator – *Communitalism*.

*   Entrepreneur Van der Coff: Corporate Integrator – *Corporate* Ecosystem; and
*   Adopter Ariyaratne: Individual–Societal Integrator – *Collective Awakening*.

*   Adventurer Branson: Eco Integrator – *Eco/service* Provider; and
*   Change Agent Johar: Civic Integrator – Impact *Hub*.

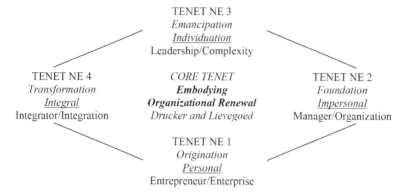

Figure 6.2 Renewal of leadership: emergent tenets

In each of the paired cases, there needs to be a meeting between self and other, as well as between "masculine" and feminine", most especially at "midlife" in the late 30s to late 40s transition, for example interconnecting "masculine" innovator with "feminine" enabler. This has nothing of course to do with "male" and "female", but rather has individual and psychological, as well as cultural connotations. For psychotherapist Carl Jung, it involved confronting the "shadow" side within you, individually and societally, with a view to enhancing integration, individually and collectively (Stephens, 1991). For us, such a "shadow" is both personal and cultural. We now turn to Chapter 7, from individual and organizational emergence towards economic and societal navigation, on the path of renewal, serving to recognize and release economic GENE-ius.

References

Beck, D. and Cowan, C. (1996) *Spiral Dynamics*. Chichester: Wiley-Blackwell.

Block, P. (1993) *Stewardship*. San Francisco, CA: Berrett-Koehler.

Drucker, P. (1977) *Management: Tasks, Analysis and Practices*. London: Pan Books.

Hawken, P. (2005) *Natural Capitalism: The Next Industrial Revolution. 10th edition.* London: Routledge.

Jaques, E. (1997) *Requisite Organization*. Farnham: Gower.

Khurana, R. (2007) *From Higher Aims to Hired Hands: The Social Transformation of the American Business Schools and the Unfulfilled Promise of Management as a Profession.* Princeton, NJ: Princeton University Press.

Koopman, A. (1991) *Transcultural Management*. Chichester: Wiley-Blackwell.

Lessem, R. (1987) *Intrapreneurship*. Aldershot: Wildwood House.

Lessem, R. (1991) *Total Quality Learning*. Chichester: Wiley-Blackwell.

Lessem, R. (1998) *Management Development through Cultural Diversity*. London: Routledge.

Lessem, R. (2016) *The Integrators: Beyond Leadership, Knowledge and Value Creation*. Abingdon: Routledge.

Lessem, R. and Palsule, S. (1997) *Managing in Four Worlds: From Competition to Cocreation*. Chichester: Wiley-Blackwell.

Lessem, R. and Schieffer, A. (2009) *Transformation Management: Toward the Integral Enterprise*. Farnham: Gower.

Lessem, R. and Schieffer, A. (2010a) *Integral Economics: Releasing the Economic Genius of your Society*. Farnham: Gower.

Lessem, R. and Schieffer, A. (2010b) *Integral Research and Innovation: Transforming Enterprise and Society*. Farnham: Gower.

Lessem, R. with Schieffer, A. (2015) *Integral Renewal: A Relational and Renewal Perspective*. Farnham: Gower.

Lievegoed, B. (1990) *The Developing Organisation*. Chichester: Wiley-Blackwell.

Moore, J. (1996) *The Death of Competition: Leadership and Strategy in the Age of Business Ecosystems*. Chichester: Wiley.

Nonaka, I. and Takeuchi, H. (1995) *The Knowledge Creating Company*. Oxford: Oxford University Press.

Parikh, J. (1996) *Managing the Self: Management by Detached Involvement*. Chichester: Wiley-Blackwell.

Pascale, R. and Athos, A. (1982) *The Art of Japanese Management*. London: Penguin.

Peters, T. and Waterman, R. (1982) *In Search of Excellence*. New York: Harper Business.

Schieffer, A. and Lessem, R. (2014a) *Integral Development: Realizing the Transformative Potential of Individuals, Organizations, Societies*. Farnham: Gower.

Schieffer, A. and Lessem, R. (2014b) *Integral Development: Transforming the Potential of Individual, Organization and Society*. Farnham: Gower.

Senge, P. (2006) *The Fifth Discipline: The Art and Practice of the Learning Organization*. New York: Random House.

Sharmer, O. and Kaufer, K. (2013) *Leading from the Emerging Future: From Ecosystem to Ecosystem Economies*. San Francisco, CA: Berrett-Koehler.

Stevens, A. (1991) *On Jung*. London: Penguin.

7 Navigating

Releasing economic GENE-ius

Summary of chapter:

1 grounded in local–global movement in which community activation is lodged;
2 emerging middle–up–down–across through awakened integral consciousness;
3 navigated through innovation driven institutionalized research embodied in an economic research and development centre;
4 commit effectively to resolve burning issues embodying integral development.

Introduction: the renewal path in effecting integral development

Four critical success factors for releasing economic GENE-ius

We now turn from emergence to navigation, on the path of *renewal*, and from the state, followed by the individual and organizational to now, most specifically, the economic-and-societal, in embodying integral development. In so doing, parallel to our inter-institutional genealogy (see Chapter 11) I revisit the conclusion to *Integral Economics: Releasing the Genius of Your Society* (Lessem and Schieffer, 2010a). At that point we alluded to four critical success factors (CSF), in releasing economic gene-ius, which we have turned into four elements of CARE, as indicated below, also as Figure 7.1:

We shall now introduce each of these factors in detail, specifically as below, which can be more or less linked with our inter-institutional genealogy, as we shall see (Chapter 11): community, sanctuary, research university and laboratory in turn.

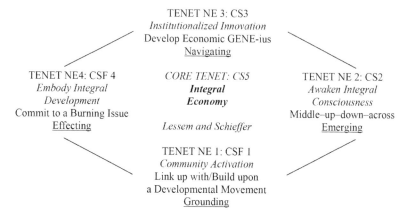

Figure 7.1 Embodiment, renewal and integral economics

1   *Grounding – community activation/build community circles*: <u>link up with</u>, build on, existing <u>local and global movements</u> for socio-economic development.
2   *Emergence – awakening integral consciousness/actualize innovation ecosystem*: maintain interconnected holistic focus, <u>middle–up–down–across</u>.
3   *Navigating – innovation driven institutionalized research/recognize inter-institutional genealogy* <u>for locating and developing economic GENE-ius</u>.
4   *Effecting – embodying integral development/effect integral enterprise and society*: <u>commit to resolving a real burning issue</u>.

Grounding: Link up with a movement – aligned with community

Community activation/create a learning community

We start with the need to link up with a local/global movement, and thereby with a particular *community* in relation to this.

The Philippine social activist and Right Livelihood Award winner Nicanor Perlas, to whom we referred in Chapter 4, in his acclaimed book *Shaping Globalisation* (2000), described the emergence of global civil society, in particular in the past twenty years, as the most significant social innovation of the last century. While by 1914 there were just a thousand NGOs (non-governmental organizations) all over the world, at the time of writing, in 2016, there are around forty thousand acting on an international

Table 7.1 Integral enterprise in society

Embodying Integral Enterprise in Society: Relational Effect *Environmentalism; culturalism; democracy; sustainability* Heal planet; peacefully co-evolve; open society; economic opportunity

- *Attributes of Embodiment* – RELATIONAL PATH: Grounding – goko personal and communal engagement; Emergence – calabash of group knowledge sharing; Navigation – GENE rhythm of social innovation; Effect – integral realities/societal transformation. RENEWAL PATH: Grounding – integral state; Emergence – institutional integration; Navigation – *releasing GENE-ius*; Effect – societal renaissance. REASONED REALIZATION PATH: Grounding – school education for all the senses; Emergence – enterprise learning and development; Navigation – sustainable development university; Effecting – institutional genealogy.
- *Integrator role*: **Lessem and Schieffer.**
- *Critical success factors underlying integral economy*: Grounded in **local–global movement** in which *community activation* is lodged; *Emerging* **middle–up–down–across** through *awakened integral consciousness*; *navigated* through *innovation driven institutionalized research* embodied in an **economic research and development centre**; *effective* through a **commitment to resolving burning issues** embodying integral development.

scale. National numbers are even higher: India alone is estimated to have between one and two million such NGOs.

Furthermore, "civil society" is an even more pervasive phenomenon than these particular NGOs, as it encompasses the plethora of civic and grassroots movements of ordinary people the world over, who feel impelled to act together to address local or global burning issues that they care about passionately. Indeed, the American environmentalist and social activist Paul Hawken called this phenomenon the "Blessed Unrest" (2007). The large-scale movement to which he refers has, for him, three basic roots – *environmental activism, social justice initiatives, and indigenous cultures' resistance to globalization* – all of which have become intertwined.

In fact, referring back to our Chapter 4, environmentalism, culturalism, democratization and sustainable development are all such developmental movements. It is in that guise that our work on *Integral Green Zimbabwe* (Mamukwa *et al.*, 2014) and on *Integral Green Slovenia* (Piciga *et al.*, 2016), in turn, represents collective efforts, involving in each case the public, private, civic and environmental sectors in such movements, most especially related to environmentalism and culturalism specifically, and to sustainable development generally.

We now turn to the second of our Critical Success Factors, aligned with Awakening integral consciousness.

Emerge: middle–up–down–across – aligned with sanctuary

Awakening integral consciousness/actualizing an innovation ecosystem

Maintain interconnected focus

From our observations and experiences around the four worlds (see Table 7.2 below), you don't build an integral economy "top down" within a macroeconomy as a whole, as in Britain or America, Zimbabwe or Slovenia. Nor do you start bottom up, with and through the people "at the bottom of the pyramid". Rather, we believe the most effective way of "releasing the economic GENE-ius" of a particular enterprise-and-society is via a "middle–up–down–across approach", be it that of a Sekem in Egypt, a Grameen in Bangladesh, a Mondragon in Spain, Canon in Japan or an Interface in the US. What does that actually mean?

A top-down approach would start with the overarching macroeconomic system, as per, for example, capitalism or socialism, both of which, for us, lack both academic–theoretical and practical–contextual integrity. In recent years, the world has been overwhelmed with the "top-down" approach of a Washington Consensus, building on the abstract fundamentals of the neo-liberal Chicago School, that is, of free markets, free trade, privatization and deregulation. Overall – witness the recent economic and financial crisis (Lessem and Schieffer, 2009) – such a top-down approach, in this case from multilateral agencies and the multinational bankers, has not worked.

On the other hand, "bottom-up" individual enterprises or communities in isolation, are by far too weak in themselves to become beacons of development. Rather, and true to an awakening of integral consciousness, starting out from a societal centre or moral core, an interconnected web of macro and micro, as illustrated by the examples in Table 7.3 below, local and global, individual and communal, academic and practical, "mesa-enterprises" (in between macro and micro), set within and across one community or society and another, provides our "middle–up–down–across" approach towards an integral economy.

This invariably involves one or more catalysts with a holistic outlook, such as Muhammad Yunus (2003) as founder of Grameen Bank or Chairman Kaku (Lessem and Schieffer, 2009) at Canon in Japan (see Table 7.3 below). Each one as such responds to a particular burning issue, builds on a particular social movement, and also *follows one economic path or another, which we have identified as either relational*

Table 7.2 Middle–up–down–across

Case	Burning issue	Path	Approach		Up	Down	Across
			Middle				
Sekem Egypt	**Material and spiritual renewal**	**Centre: moral economic core**	Abouleish founder, with family, employees, local community, national and international support		Fusion of cultural and religious perspectives: Islam and an-throposophy, Orient and Occident / economics of love	Building up of Sekem from the (desert) ground; revitalization of the ground (Sekem meaning: vitality of the sun)	Spreading of the Sekem-way: from food to clothing to health products / establishing a university for sustainability
Grameen Bangladesh	**Alleviate poverty, economic inclusion**	**Southern economic path: self-sufficient economy**	Yunus economics professor, with students and local women		Micro-finance theory, linked to social context in rural communities	Experi-mentation on the ground; building a bank for the poor with the poor	Expanding the new approach to all sectors of society (clothing, health, telecom etc.)
Canon Japan	**Address global imbalance**	**Eastern economic path: develop-mental economy**	Kaku chairman, with all Canon employees		Meta-philosophy "kyosei", rooted in Japan's cultural grounds	Implement the "kyosei"-philosophy in Canon	Connecting keretisu-style with every stakeholder including suppliers, customers, community
Mondragon Spain	**Promote social justice**	**Northern economic path: social economy**	Arizmendi Catholic priest, with local workers		Distribu-tivism / design of the worker cooperative, rooted in previous cultural and social designs in Basque country	Building Mondragon up, together with local workers, continuously co-evolving the underlying theory and practice	Expanding in other industries, including a university; connecting with Basque community at large
Interface USA	**Restore the Earth**	**Western economic path: living economy**	Anderson with all employees and clients		Literature on sustainability / new enterprise design	Back to the roots / learning from nature / taking every employee on the journey	Becoming a role model / active sharing of knowledge / initiating a movement

Critical Success Factor 2: towards an integral economy

(self-sufficiency), renewal (developmental economy), reason (social economy) or realization (living economy).

Starting from your moral core: middle–up–down–across development

It is important that you, on behalf of your individual self, your institution, your community or society – in each case starting from your moral core (whereby we have genealogically aligned this second CSF with a *Sanctuary*) – identify what equivalent middle–up–down–across approach you can build upon.

Each of you, individually, institutionally and societally, will have a particular pre-emphasis as we have identified in our approach to *Integral Economy* (Lessem and Schieffer, 2010a), on either a self-sufficient, a developmental, a social or a living economy, together with the revitalization of a relevant, thereby sanctuary-laden, moral economic core, or indeed cores. Your emphasis will depend on a range of complex factors, for example, on whether your economy is urban or rural, highly industrialized or otherwise, high tech or low tech. But, as illustrated earlier, it will also depend on the particular burning issue you identify in your context. Now we turn to the third Critical Success Factor, that is, the need for innovation driven, institutionalized social research.

Navigation: integral economy – aligned with academy

Innovation driven institutional research/inter-institutional genealogy

Towards an integral economic research university

Throughout our work we have been very critical of the academic discipline of economics, at least the narrowly neo-liberal and duly universalized version that currently prevails. As a result, through our integral approach to economics and enterprise we have developed an overarching research agenda – involving both integral method and content – as well as undergraduate and postgraduate curricula, encompassing nature and culture, technology and enterprise (Lessem and Schieffer, 2010b, 2015). Moreover, this is invariably grounded in a particular local community, emerging locally–globally in relation to others, thereafter navigated newly globally, and ultimately effected globally–locally. *Integral Economics, then, as we see it, can provide an overriding framework for engaging with the rich diversity of economic thinking, and practice, from the four corners of the globe, with a view to releasing the GENE-ius of each society and economy.*

Indeed, through the rhythmical GENE-ius built into the four economic paths introduced, the "student of economics", as an academic researcher or as a business, governmental or civic practitioner, is invited to both empathetically and also critically engage with the economic context of their society, both in theory and in practice. At the same time, we acknowledge the limitations of any academically based framework, however well it accommodates the complexity of the context it is modelling, and however much it enables you to engage in practical application.

Academy as integral part of a genealogy

As we shall see with our inter-institutional genealogy (see Chapter 11), we recast universities (navigating) as part of an integral genealogical whole, including local community (grounding), local–global sanctuary (emergence) and global–local laboratory (effecting). Universities as such as a whole (there are of course rare exceptions) do not function as centres for societal renewal, though the best of them, like MIT or Stanford in the US, or Cambridge and Oxford in the UK, are research centres of note in the natural sciences. When it comes to the humanities and the social sciences these universities are rarely such developmental agents, because social knowledge is commonly lodged in particular communities locally, if not also religious and spiritual sources locally–globally, from which universities are all too often markedly detached (communities) or indeed overly attached (religions).

Vital to our overall, integral cause, then, is innovation driven, institutionalized social research, duly enriched by relevant humanities. What then, ultimately, are we seeking to *effect*?

Commit to a burning issue: aligned with a social laboratory

Embodying integral development/integral enterprise and society

Burning issue and relevant path to releasing GENE-ius

The approach that we take, as you have seen, and that is intrinsic to our integral orientation, involves focusing on the socio-economic issue (or issues) of utmost concern in your particular context, and taking this burning issue, combined with the unique gifts and capacities you hold, as a starting point for releasing economic GENE-ius. This is very different from a conventional academic, religious or even communal approach, and should be the role of a genealogical laboratory.

When it comes to laboratories in the social sciences, however, these are virtually non-existent, paling into insignificance when compared with such laboratories, whether academic, governmental or corporate, in the technology-oriented natural sciences. Unfortunately, moreover, most universities focus on individual education, as well as individual social research, often disconnected from the burning issues faced in reality, and in a particular community or society. This is particularly damaging in

Table 7.3 Releasing economic GENE-ius

Four critical success factors in integral economic development
1) Join existing local and global movements for socio-economic transformation
• *Leverage your individual, organizational and communal ecosystemic efforts by linking up with local and global movements that are relevant for your particular economic path and moral economic core.*
2) Maintain interconnected focus: moving middle–up–down–across
• *The economy does not work mechanically and in linear fashion, but resembles a highly complex living system. Hence any approach towards economic renewal requires you to build an interconnected web of macro and micro, local and global, individual and communal, academic and practical, elements.*
3) Release economic GENE-ius via innovation driven institutionalized research
• *Join, or set up with others, individually and collectively, a social research institute that in itself is a centre of local economic renewal, and that:*
○ *contributes to an integral understanding of economics;*
○ *addresses the challenge of designing economic and business research and development/curricula, requisite to the natural, cultural, social and financial complexity of the economy and enterprise in your society;*
○ *engages with the rich diversity of economic thinking from all over the world, philosophically and contextually, in theory and practice;*
○ *becomes a catalyst of economic renewal, co-engaging enterprises and communities in your society;*
○ *is linked to other integral economic laboratories in the world.*
4) Commit to a burning issue and the most relevant integral economic path
• *Focus on the economic issue that is of utmost concern in your particular context, and take this to be a starting point for releasing economic GENE-ius.*
• *The long-term commitment to such needs to be sourced in moral inspiration that is relevant and authentic to yourself and your particular context, and, at the same time, enriched by a compelling universal truth.*

"developing" societies. This "being out of touch with reality" is for us a core reason why economic education, in the way that it is conventionally offered, has become increasingly irrelevant for today's world in general, and for a particular world, be it that of Ghana or Germany, specifically.

I-U-S: synergizing particular moral inspiration and universal truth

In all cases we reviewed, of would-be integral enterprises and economies, the long-term commitment to a burning issue, which sustains efforts to build a new kind of "relevant" enterprise, requires a strong moral inspiration. For Ibrahim Abouleish's Sekem Group, in Egypt for example, it is to reclaim the desert and restore the earth, drawing on "the vitality of the sun" (meaning of Sekem; Abouleish, 2005). Such an inspiration has to be relevant and authentic to the core protagonists and to the particular context, and, at the same time, it needs to be enriched by a compelling universal truth, in this case aligned with the overarching principles of ecology.

For Muchineripi und Kada of Chinyika (Lessem *et al.*, 2013), the moral inspiration came out of the acknowledgement of "I am an African" and the rediscovery of the wisdom engrained in their indigenous belief and knowledge systems. The universal truth, at the same time, to which they equally opened themselves, was that of the global logic of contemporary agricultural production methods. In the process, both aspects, the local and the global, were enriched; and the dialectic between "local wisdom and global knowledge" is at the heart of the moral economic core.

We are now ready to conclude.

Conclusion: the future economy is integral

In conclusion, then, as we have seen, there are four critical success factors, pertaining to the release of your particular economic GENE-ius, as a community or society, in effecting integral development, most especially, through not exclusively, on the path of renewal (see Table 7.3).

We next turn to an unlikely but rather remarkable societal case for our final effective and transformative embodiment of integral development, on now the path of renewal, and that is Oman in the Gulf.

References

Abouleish, I. (2005) *Sekem: A Sustainable Community in the Egyptian Desert.* Edinburgh: Floris Publications.

Hawken, P. (2007) *Blessed Unrest: How The Largest Movement In The World Came Into Being.* New York: Penguin.

Lessem, R. and Schieffer, A. (2009) *Transformation Management: Towards the Integral Enterprise*. Farnham: Gower.

Lessem, R. and Schieffer, A. (2010a) *Integral Economics: Releasing the Genius of Your Society*. Abingdon: Routledge.

Lessem, R. and Schieffer, A. (2010b) *Integral Research and Innovation: Transforming Enterprise and Society*. Abingdon: Routledge.

Lessem, R. and Schieffer, A. (2015) *Integral Renewal: A Relational and Renewal Perspective*. Abingdon: Routledge.

Lessem, R., Muchineripi, P. and Kada, S. (2013) *Integral Community: Political Economy to Social Commons*. Abingdon: Routledge.

Mamukwa, E., Lessem, R. and Schieffer, A. (2014) *Integral Green Zimbabwe: An African Phoenix Rising*. Farnham: Gower.

Perlas, N. (2000) *Shaping Globalisation: Civil Society, Cultural Power and Threefolding*. Cape Town: Kima Global Publishers.

Piciga, D., Schieffer, A. and Lessem, R. (2016) *Integral Green Slovenia: Towards a Social Knowledge and Value Based Society and Economy at the Heart of Europe*. Abingdon: Routledge.

Yunus, M. (2003) *Banker to the Poor: The Story of Grameen Bank*. New York: Aurum Press.

8   Effecting

Bridging the gulf – societal renaissance

Summary of chapter:

1   grounded relationally in the Arab, Swahili and Balochi worlds;
2   emerging renewal wise through this, and in blending tradition and modernity;
3   navigating reason wise though shura-based democracy;
4   effecting realization through distributed oil revenues.

Introduction: the reasoned path to effecting integral development

Oman and its Sultan

In this concluding chapter on the path of *renewal*, thereby *effecting* the embodiment of integral development, through an overall Omani *societal renaissance*, I want to attempt a creative synthesis of all of *CARE*-and-CARE, on the path of renewal. Such a synthesis lies, for the African philosopher Ali Mazrui (1986), at the heart of an evolving civilization. For our purposes, it ultimately embodies integral development, contextualized within a particular society, in this case reflecting overall but also in conjunction with the other relational and renewal paths, the path of reasoned realization. Moreover, whereas the previous chapter had a strong economic emphasis, this one, on Oman, is more culturally and politically oriented.

The society we have chosen, then, perhaps surprisingly – because Oman has kept itself below the radar for so many years – for illustration, is situated at the geographical cross-roads between the Arabian Peninsula, Africa and Asia. Materially and spiritually in close contact with the African south and the Asian east, Oman has also drawn on the European north and Anglo-Saxon west, thereby *bridging the Gulf*, so to speak, in its location alongside

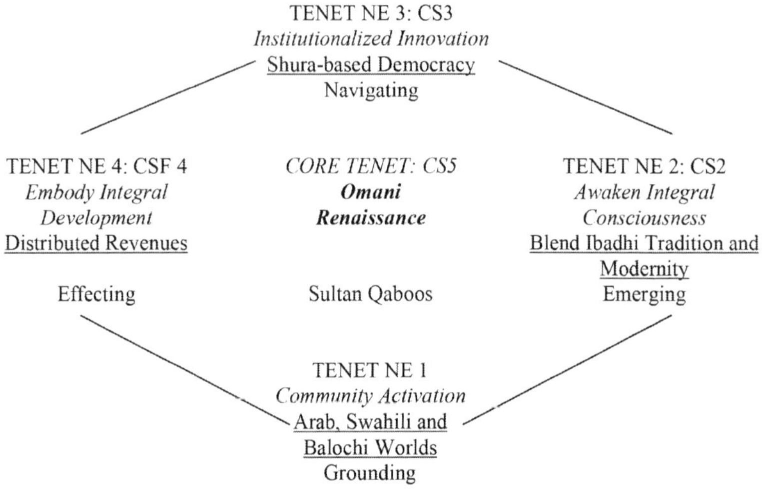

TENET NE 3: CS3
Institutionalized Innovation
Shura-based Democracy
Navigating

TENET NE 4: CSF 4
Embody Integral
Development
Distributed Revenues

Effecting

CORE TENET: CS5
Omani
Renaissance

Sultan Qaboos

TENET NE 2: CS2
Awaken Integral
Consciousness
Blend Ibadhi Tradition and
Modernity
Emerging

TENET NE 1
Community Activation
Arab, Swahili and
Balochi Worlds
Grounding

Figure 8.1 Embody integral development in Oman: renewal path

the Gulf States, indeed bordered by Saudi Arabia and the Yemen. In fact, over the course of four and a half decades, there has been a social and economic transformation in the whole of Oman, spearheaded by the remarkable Sultan Qaboos bin Said, who ascended to the throne in 1970.

Table 8.1 Bridging the gulf

Embodying Integral Development: Effecting Integral Embodiment   ***Oman: bridging the gulf on the renewal path***   Omani integral societal advantage

- *Attributes of embodiment* – RELATIONAL PATH: Grounding – Goko personal and communal engagement; Emergence – calabash of group knowledge sharing; Navigation – GENE rhythm of social innovation; Effect – integral realities/societal transformation. RENEWAL PATH: Grounding – *integral state*; Emergence – institutional integration; Navigation – releasing GENE-ius; Effect – *societal renaissance*. REASONED REALIZATION PATH: Grounding – school education for all the senses; Emergence – enterprise learning and development; Navigation – sustainable development university; Effecting – institutional genealogy.
- *Integrator role*: e.g., ***Sultan Qaboos.***
- *Genealogical institute*: *grounded relationally* in the ***Arab, Swahili and Balochi*** worlds; *emerging renewal wise* through such, and in the blending of ***Ibadhi tradition and "western" modernity***; *navigating reason wise* though ***shura-based democracy***; *effecting realization* through ***distributed oil revenues.***

Reformer on the throne

As we shall see, Qaboos not only pursued overall CARE, societally, but also remained true to his unique self (Sultan Qaboos) and to his royal dynasty (Said al Said), drawing on the formative influences of those who had come before. In reaching out to others, he has drawn institutionally upon specifically "north-western" English influences, but has generally immersed himself in the music of all spheres: Arabic and Asian, African and European. We shall now review how he has pursued these, drawing altogether on the marvellous biography *The Reformer on the Throne* (2004) by Sergei Plekhanov, who is currently Associate Professor of Political Science at York University in Canada.

Grounding integral development in nature and community

Omani people: Arab/Swahili/Balochi

On 18 November 1940, the then Omani Sultan's wife, Miyzun bin Ahmed Alma'ashani, gave birth to a son, Qaboos. As he grew up and learned to read and write, one of the first questions to arouse the curiosity of the young Sayyid was why his country was named Oman. Arab cultures had long since merged with the black tribes there, creating a strange world that spoke Swahili and danced to torrid African rhythms. Oman also had a large contingent of Balochi peoples. Balochi speakers live mainly in an area now composed of parts of south-eastern Iran and south-western Pakistan that was once the historic region of Balochistan. They also live in Central Asia (near Merv, Turkmenistan) and south-western Afghanistan.

Oman's nature: touched by four seas

Qaboos then, for Plekhanov, loved exploring the geography of his Oman. One of his chief pleasures was to study books and maps, travelling in his imagination from Omani town to town. Stories about different parts of Oman enthralled him as much as history lessons. He was naturally drawn to the ordinary Omani people. While encounters with those of the royal entourage were predictable and therefore lacking much interest, his encounters with desert dwellers, fishermen and merchants were far more rewarding. He was avid to learn about his people and the country and quickly realized that these were the best teachers.

Oman is a land that is at once beautiful and mysterious. Its beauty is bound up in a collage of towering mountain ranges, highlands, regions rendered fertile by intricate water systems, and deserts. Oman's coastline is touched by four seas – the Gulf, the Arabian Sea, the Gulf of Oman and the Indian Ocean. A richly diverse terrain is captured vividly in Oman's mountain ranges with their jagged and angry profiles, rocks that are folded and pleated like some exotic garment, rock faces that are veritable interwoven tapestries of multicoloured minerals, or cascades of mountains and hills that dissolve into the distant horizon in rhythmic undulation. Aside from his love of the exploration of nature, Qaboos was also engaged with the spirit of his Omani place, that is, with the spirit of Islam.

Emerging development from a cultural and spiritual sanctuary

Qaboos' spiritual fulcrum

Thoughts about life, about relations between people and ultimately with God, began to interest the royal child at an early age. Among the many books he read, a collection of Shakespeare's tragedies compiled by an Arab writer impressed him most. He was already reaching out from the local to the global, albeit in this specifically English context. Having learned to read at five, the future Sultan enjoyed immersing himself in a complex world of human passions. But the most important book that the heir to the throne discovered for himself was the Holy Qur'an. At every stage of his life it has been his spiritual fulcrum. In fact, from its eighth-century inception, Omani Ibadhi (as a third alternative to Sunni and Shi'a) democracy, according to UAE UNESCO ambassador Hussein Ghubash (2006), then set out to obey as faithfully as possible the values of a moderate, tolerant Islam. To that end it was structured in the framework of the imama around seven basic pillars: the principle of al-ijma (consensus) and al-shura (consultation); the principle of the free election of the imam; al-dustur, the constitution; al-majalis, the institution of the imama; the principle of the independence of the law/ equality before the law; the law of zakat (legal alms); and the suppression of the army in times of peace.

Giving people a voice in their destiny

Qaboos' great predecessor, Said bin Sultan (1806–1856), realized that the state could only be strengthened by enlarging the base of political power. He therefore created the Sultan's Council, which included representatives of different classes. When he ascended to the throne, Sultan Qaboos started his tours around the country, lasting several weeks, inaugurating consultations with local people from all walks of life. The former Said bin Sultan, well aware of the fact that in an autocracy the real power belongs to those who have access to the ruler, decided to make himself as accessible as possible.

The beauty of calligraphy

The young Sultan-to-be had been christened "Qaboos", a rare name in the Arab world, and the title of Sayyid (His Highness) indicated his unique destiny as a future ruler of his people. In his early years he was brought up in the green south of the country, in a place called, melodically, Salalah.

The library at the palace in Salalah holds a large collection of books, some of great antiquity. The beauty of the calligraphy in those ancient books is in itself an aid to contemplation, and it would have been natural for the young Sayyid to gaze at the exquisite characters and long to understand their meaning. As his understanding developed, the very first lines of each "*sura*", or verse from the Qur'an, arranged so carefully, would have captured his attention with their concepts of singular wisdom.

However, he was to draw not only on this longstanding, spiritual and historical tradition, but also on the more immediate dynasty from which he hailed.

The rise and fall of a traditional dynasty

Most modern historians agree on 1744 as the date of birth of the dynasty from which Qaboos was descended, with the investiture of Ahmed bin Said (1744–84). This was the fifth dynasty since the beginning of the Islamic period, the previous five having faded out through failing to curb the tribal element in Oman. For the young Qaboos, the figure of his great ancestor was of particular importance. Though separated by two centuries, they had much in common. For Ahmed, like Qaboos, came to power after many years of administrative decay. Devastation and misery surrounded both of them.

Qaboos studied all the facets of Said bin Sultan's political life, because, from an early age, he dreamed of matching his nineteenth-century ancestor's great triumphs. As he explored the character and policies of his two great ancestors, he found that both had a capacity to dream, and a passionate desire to realize their dreams, combined with a more-than-common intelligence and competence. When Said bin Sultan died on board of the *Victoria* en route from Muscat to Zanzibar, which had become his second home, his empire was flourishing. Who could have thought that, not many years after his death, not even a trace would be left of that glory and that the Omani empire would be once more driven by war and revolt?

Fusion of cultural horizons: Sandhurst to Salalah

In the autumn of 1960, Qaboos was sent to Sandhurst, the UK's pre-eminent military training establishment. After lessons in the classroom and the parade ground, or after several hours in the library, Qaboos liked to sit alone in his room and daydream, listening to music. One of his favourite pieces was Händel's *Water Music*.

Qaboos felt that Händel's music identified the unchanging essence at the heart of British culture, something sensed by Händel in 1717, and by Qaboos now. Songs and melodies from many native lands found a place at Sandhurst, and commanders and teachers made no class distinctions among their cadets, whether British or foreign. When he completed his training at Sandhurst, Qaboos chose to broaden his European exposure by taking up a post with the British army in Germany.

Music of the different spheres: art and culture

Qaboos was accustomed to learning things thoroughly, so he was not satisfied with a superficial acquaintance with Germany and its culture. He admired the compositions of Bach and Brahms, but although music can communicate the emotions of the soul across cultures and languages, Qaboos recognized the necessity of learning at least elementary German if he was to gain a political understanding of the country.

After his stay in Germany, he proceeded onto a three-month world trip. He was overwhelmed with enthusiasm and reverence for the power and originality of ancient cultures. He photographed ancient monuments and ruins, trying to imagine scenes of modern life against this background. He continued to be attracted by a combination of art and culture. Then it was time to return to Oman.

The destiny of monarchy in a modern world

After his experiences in England and in other progressive countries, it was difficult for Sayyid Qaboos to adjust to the confined atmosphere of a huge family ruled by a form of extreme paternalism. The whole of Oman was the family and the Sultan, his father, was the stern paterfamilias. All subjects were considered as children under his personal supervision. Moreover, in December 1963, the independence of Zanzibar was proclaimed, black nationalists ousted the last Sultan there, and an atrocious massacre ensued, resulting in the death of some 20,000 Arabs.

Sayyid Qaboos' return to Oman coincided with the Zanzibar tragedy, and he constantly thought about the destiny of monarchy in the modern world:

is it capable of resisting extremist forces armed not only with guns but also with populist slogans of equality and prosperity? Oman seemed unable to shake off the country's drowsiness. And Qaboos, while he had spent many years immersed in his country's culture and history, was prepared to take over command from his increasingly disinterested father.

Spiritual heritage and open future

The opportunity came in July 1970, when his father was deposed and the young Sultan's declaration spread through the country at the speed of lightning:

> *"My first act will be the immediate abolition of all the unnecessary restrictions on your daily lives. My people, I will proceed without delay to transform your life into a prosperous one with a bright future. Every one of you must play your part toward this goal. Our country in the past was famous and strong. If we work in unity and cooperation, we will regenerate that glorious past and we will take our rightful place in the world. We hope that this day will mark the beginning of a new age and a great future for us all. The government and the people are one body. If one of its limbs fails to do its duty, the other parts of the body will suffer. We hope that you will think well of us and at the same time we hope that we shall think well of you."* (Plekhanov, 2004)

Qaboos had spent many years studying the spiritual heritage and history of Oman. He knew his country deeply, but all his knowledge was filtered as though by a screen through which no more than a glimpse of the present actuality could be seen, and through which he was completely invisible to his people. Now his country was lying open before him, and he, too, was no longer hidden from view.

Navigate integral development: research, education and polity

Building an Omani-style democracy

Every day, immediately after he assumed power, Qaboos faced new problems in need of urgent attention. His father had led the state into deep crisis, and it was difficult at times to decide which problem was the most pressing. On top of all the internal problems, the country had to break into the international arena to re-establish itself in the diplomatic field. Qaboos invited representatives of many other countries to come and visit Oman in order to see the country and place relations on an equal footing. The first attempt to carry out the monarch's overall plans comprised the creation of a Provisional Consultative Council, born in effect out of the prior research Qaboos had conducted, especially into the life and work of Said bin Sultan.

The difficulty of the transformation, though, was that it had to be undertaken with such urgency, and that everything had to be done simultaneously.

Promoting "Ilm Laden Education"

A great merit of Qaboos bin Said's approach was his respectful attitude towards the customs and culture of all of the peoples in the country. In the absence of a "spiritual infrastructure", the reforms could not have had a solid base. For Qaboos:

> *"Each country goes through periods of progress and decline. We had to find a way of renewal, but funds from the sale of oil alone could not do that. Education is a key to success. It is not an end in itself; it is a means, first of all to self-knowledge. Without education people cannot distinguish good from evil, cannot take care of themselves."*
> (Plekhanov, 2004)

As such, he was only too aware of the role that knowledge had played in the heyday of Muslim societies, in the ninth to fourteenth centuries. In Islam, the pursuit of knowledge is acknowledged as a basic, God-given, human instinct. It fulfils the person in his/her quest for truth and confers greater insight into the workings of nature, thereby strengthening the relationship between man and God. The much-quoted aphorism "for even knowledge itself is power", first articulated by Frances Bacon, was implicit in the earliest teachings of Islam. It was given practical expression in the establishment of schools, academies, libraries and observatories in the main Islamic centres of learning throughout the world.

Given a new lease of life

Another top priority for Oman had been the creation of a modern health service. Omanis have literally and metaphorically been given a new lease of life – the average lifespan in Oman nowadays is 72 years, whereas thirty years ago it was a mere 50 years. Every major facility built in Oman in the first years of Qaboos bin Said's rule caused a revolution in some sphere of life: an international airport in Seeb in 1973; a television station in Muscat in 1974; power stations and desalination plants; modern roads connecting the capital with the other cities. All this swiftly and dramatically changed a lifestyle established over centuries.

Shura to Majalis al-Astishari: consultation to democracy

In contrast to the reformers of many other countries, Qaboos always aimed to draw out the creative potential of the traditional structures, whose roots reach deep into the past. Over the past quarter of a century, numerous laws and codes defining relations in the economic and social spheres have been adopted. And although "shari'a" has remained the foundation of Omani legislation, the promulgation of what has been termed Basic Law has completed the creation of the legislative system. Such a Law bestowed by the Sultan defines the fundamental principles of state policy, and also the system of forming authoritative institutions. For the first time in the nation's history, the Sultan's prerogatives, as well as the mechanisms for the functioning of the monarchy and for the transfer of power, are underlined. In 1982 the Sultan promulgated a decree establishing the State Consultative Council (SCC = "Majalis al-Astishari") made up of 17 members representing the "wilayats", 17 state officials and 11 members from the private sector. In his speech he said:

> *"While we entrust your Council with the duty of giving opinions and advice, it should also be the framework for a joint effort between government and public sectors for studying the aims and dimensions of our development plans, the priorities fixed for their projects and the obstacles which stand in the way of implementing these plans, and suitable solutions for them."* (Plekhanov, 2004)

The membership of the SCC was completely replaced every two years. Its members made many tours of the country, meeting the *walis* and other representatives of the people, a strategy that permitted an objective analysis of the government's actions and an evaluation of the efficiency of the development program. The Council has also become a kind of school of politics for the subjects of Sultan Qaboos, as television eventually began to broadcast their discussions. In 1991, the SCC was replaced by the Consultative Council ("Majilis al-Shura"). The Islamic principle of "shura" was made the foundation of its activity. The most authoritative people in the Sultanate were permitted to vote for nominees to membership of the Council. Representatives of the government were no longer automatically granted seats on it. Three years later, elections for the "Majalis" were held. In a major break with tradition, two women entered the chamber of people's representatives for the first time. The Council was enlarged to 80 members.

The third Majalis al-Dawla was elected in 1997. For the President of this council:

> *"The creation of the Majalis al-Dawla is the last phase of building a system of organisation. There was a need for a body that would evaluate the results of the government's activity, that would help the government. Then came the moment for a specialized independent body that would evaluate what had been done over the previous thirty years, to use the positive results for the future and avoid the negative ones. The most prominent, well prepared and well educated representatives of Omani society make up the Council, having worked in all spheres of statecraft: they have been ministers, vice-ministers, ambassadors."*
> (Plekhanov, 2004)

The transforming effect of integral development: economic laboratory

Husbanding social, economic and natural resources

Oil, meanwhile, has been the basis of economic development in Oman from the very beginning of the Omani renaissance. Having begun in 1967 with average daily production of 300,000 barrels per day, by 2000 the average daily production had risen to over 900,000 barrels. However, in contrast to its neighbours, Oman could never count on massive profits from oil and therefore must husband its resources carefully in order to fulfil its development programme, while promoting a process of continual experimentation, with a view to its economic diversification from its oil and petroleum base.

Traditional and modern

Oman, today, in the new millennium, is both a traditional and a modern society. And it has avoided the pitfalls of societies that have experienced rapid and far-reaching change – especially depersonalization and standardization. This is what makes the renaissance initiated by Sultan Qaboos unique. His personality, his aesthetic inclinations and his loyalty to historic traditions and religious values have been the most important factors of this velvet revolution. In the process of renewal, care has been taken not to damage the natural environment. Hundreds of historic forts, mosques, palaces and public buildings have been preserved. The modern architecture of Oman also pays the greatest respect to its own national traditions. However, care for the environment, as Sultan Qaboos has often stressed, has to be an international, as well as a national concern. In both national and international cases, the past needed to be brought into the future, via the present.

For Sultan Qaboos:

> *"The observance of our religious and cultural traditions is deeply embedded in the life of our country and our people, and it provides them with a comprehensive reference and guidelines within which to lead their lives – both with respect to religious observance and in their secular activities. Many years ago I told my people that they should be ready to accept what is good from the modern world, but reject those influences from it which are bad; this I feel we have succeeded in doing."* (Plekhanov, 2004)

In other words, modernization, including the development of a sound political, economic, educational and communications infrastructure, has been built upon traditional forms, rather than displacing them. This is unique to the Arab world, and with the recent exception of Japan it is unique in the world generally; it serves to bring about, at least in this specific Omani case, a genuine Arabic renaissance.

Conclusion: the conductor and his orchestra

The might of this modern nation is commanded, for Plekhanov (2004), by a man sitting out of sight in his crimson tent. In this austere setting where long ago Imams judged tribal disputes and discussed the finer points of "fikh" (jurisprudence and religious law) with lawmakers, investment projects worth hundreds of millions of dollars are today being considered. They include plans for a large-scale domestic internet network, the development of modern metallurgical and chemical production, and the laying of a gas pipeline on the bottom of the Indian Ocean.

Plekhanov (2004) writes, "Just by seeing and listening to the Sultan in person, you begin to understand the nature of his policies more deeply. He is a personality who brings artistry to everything he touches. He has established his own classical orchestra in Oman, being unique in the region". Music is almost as important to the Sultan as politics:

> *"I like many European composers, for example Sibelius, Brahms, Bach, Elgar and Olsen. But I also enjoy folk music from different countries and continents – Polish, Rumanian, and Arab melodies. I like the music of Andalucia, Turkish and Iranian music, a lot of Indian and African music. Of course I love music from other African countries, and in particular from the Yemen."*

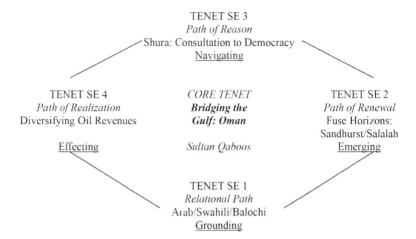

TENET SE 3
Path of Reason
Shura: Consultation to Democracy
Navigating

TENET SE 4
Path of Realization
Diversifying Oil Revenues

Effecting

CORE TENET
Bridging the
Gulf: Oman

Sultan Qaboos

TENET SE 2
Path of Renewal
Fuse Horizons:
Sandhurst/Salalah
Emerging

TENET SE 1
Relational Path
Arab/Swahili/Balochi
Grounding

Figure 8.2 Embodying integral reasoned development

Overall then, and as such, Oman is *grounded relationally in the Arab, Swahili and Balochi worlds; emerges renewal wise through these worlds, and in blending Ibadhi tradition and "western" modernity; navigates reason wise though shura-based democracy; effects realization through distributed oil revenues.*

We now turn from the relational path and that of renewal, to reasoned realization, from grounding to effect, thereby ultimately embodying integral development, of self, community, organization and society, via individual and collective learning.

References

Ghubash, H. (2006) *Oman: The Islamic Democratic Tradition.* Abingdon: Routledge.

Mazrui, A. (1986) *The Africans: A Triple Heritage.* London. BBC Books.

Plekhanov, S. (2004) *The Reformer on the Throne.* London: Trident Press.

Part III

Realization path

Institutional research to embody development

9 Grounding
Education for all the senses

Summary of chapter:

1 grounded in nature and human being – influence on community from seed to seed, building self-sufficiency;
2 emergence through constant evolution via increasing awareness, of self and heritage, sensitive to the present and connecting to the future;
3 navigating through learning and value-based creation of knowledge and wisdom, incorporating didactic games, publications, e-staffroom;
4 leveraging effective impact through CARE centre, actively engaged with communities, galvanized by European Social Fund.

Introduction: the reasoned-realization path of embodiment

An ethical education

We now turn to the "north-western" path of reasoned realization via Otona Župančiča Slovenska Bistrica Kindergarten, in Slovenia (Piciga *et al.*, 2016), for the grounding of individual, and now also communal embodiment of integral development, as revealed here by its Principal Ivana Leskovar and core faculty Karin Lavin, Mojca Pešak and Stanka Stegn. After grounding such ultimately "reasoned realization" in pre-school education, thereby originally drawing on all the senses, we shall turn to an emergent foundational focus on enterprise learning and development (MedLabs Group, Jordan), thereafter to an emancipatory genealogy (community, sanctuary, academy, laboratory), and ultimately to our overall transformative integral enterprise, economy and society, again in Slovenia (effect). While it might seem unlikely at this originating point of grounding to feature a pre-school kindergarten, this particular one is spread across some 28 sites in a central region of Slovenia. It is thereby a key feature of the country's educational and developmental infrastructure, serving to educate all the senses, and providing a model, for the country, of "ethical education", whereby, as its head teacher Leskovar says:

> *The key principles and goals of preschool education are based on the findings that a child perceives and understands the world as a whole, that he/she develops and learns in active connection with its social environment, that the interaction with peers and adults, which he/ she experiences in kindergarten, develops his/her social aspect and individuality.* (Kocijančič, 2002)

The kindergarten did not become a centre of activity, as such, overnight. It had already been breaking fresh ground in the past. In the 1970s, it was a pioneer in pre-school education. By the 1990s, moreover, it had started on the path to what by now it is terming "social innovation" with a so-called *Step by Step* program (Korak Za Korakom). The project was introduced to Slovenian primary schools by the Educational Research Institute in Ljubljana. Indeed, by 1995, George Soros' Open Society Institute in Slovenia had started implementing a program for young people, *creating conditions for learning, thereby developing one's own capabilities and skills, enabling choice, and allowing one to care for oneself, other people and the environment*, to be critical, to develop the desire to learn, to experience new things and to be open for change (Soros, 2000). In this way, *the program prepared the youngest generation of citizens for our present-day challenges in developed societies.*

Towards Integral Green Slovenia

Otona Župančiča Slovenska Bistrica, in the new millennium moreover, has been a key contributor to the *Integral Green Slovenia* Citizens' Initiative, which we described in detail in our previous volume *Innovation Driven Institutional Research*, and which we shall return to in our final chapter here. In Figure 9.1 below, we can see how the kindergarten's actions-and-reflections represent all spheres of Slovenia, as has been articulated by Slovenian coordinator of the Integral Green Citizens' Initiative Piciga, locally, and by Lessem and Schieffer (2010), globally. *The focus is placed on fellow humans, nature and community, embodied in concern for the landscape and in continuous human development. Valuing nature and our humanity represents by far the kindergarten's most important guidelines*, while its mission is to be at the centre of such value-creating activities and to be an important stakeholder in the community.

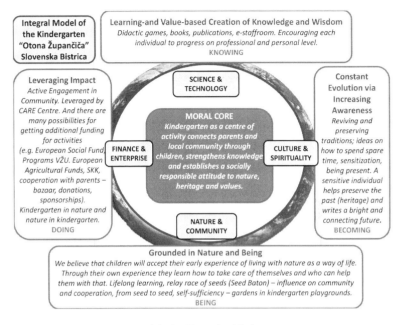

Figure 9.1 Integral green model of a Slovenian kindergarten

As it moves forwards, the kindergarten asks itself: How should we function in order to make the kindergarten a centre of local if not also national activity? After reaching a certain level of trust and cooperation in our communities, how do we continuously improve what we accomplish with them without asking too much or losing trust? Why is it important that a kindergarten becomes the integral centre of "green" economic and societal activity, and what specifically can we offer the local community?

With that overall end in mind, we start with "southern" grounding.

Grounded in nature and being in *relational* community

The Earth is calling for our help

As an illustration of grounding, and "being" with, in nature and community, to begin with, the Bistrica's Vrečkica (Bag) project was introduced in Holland and Belgium and at the Gornja Radgona fair as an example of best practice. The project dealt with the problem of plastic bags and included children, parents, all employees and a broader local community in addressing this. In cooperation with the local puppet theatre Koruzno zrno, the kindergarten's teachers prepared a puppet show on the topic of Mesečeve sanje (Moon's Dreams). The co-author of the accompanying storybook, which was also financed through this project, is also the co-author of this particular chapter, Mojca Pešak. The puppet show was performed for all children from the kindergarten and its parents. After each show, children decorated their own fabric bag. Later on, the kindergarten also participated in the contest, organized by the local utility company Komunala Slovenska Bistrica, focused on looking for the best "eco-title" for a fabric bag.

The title "Earth is calling for help!" won. Many bags were printed that could be used for the project. Since then six years have passed and the progress made in the kindergarten's local communities is visible. The media helped by informing the public about the problem and today we can still see people shopping with the bags that were decorated by the children. In all projects, the kindergarten tried to continue with the activities after the project had officially ended. Every now and then it performed the puppet show for its citizens, as a continuing reminder that Slovenians had to treat nature carefully. And at the time of writing plastic bags have been almost completely abolished in the country.

Indeed, pre-school children transferred this environmental awareness through this project into their families. Additionally, the kindergarten initiated separated waste disposal. In fact many parents indicated that their children informed them about how to separate waste. Such an ecological focus, overall moreover, led on to raising awareness against excessive consumerism. The kindergarten organized on an ongoing basis an exchange of children's clothes, toys and sports items that were thereby recycled. Exchanging such items, which the children had grown out of, and taking only what one needs, did not have only financial benefits – it was also good for the environment.

Circulating goods, money and responsibility locally

Altogether, then, the kindergarten was raising awareness and educating its children and parents in sustainable development. In fact the easiest way to reach parents is when they have small children. During the pre-school period the parents are most involved and open to change. *Locally produced food, which is bought by the kindergarten, has many layers of influence. The producers get a regular customer, paid for by the local community and parents.* The money circulates and stays with us; therefore the kindergarten in its community can decide, as it were, what to plant or to sow.

Table 9.1 Education of all the senses

Embodying Integral Development: Reasoned Realization Integral Green Slovenia: education of all the *senses* Otona Župančiča Bistrica Slovenska Taking Integral CARE
• *Attributes of embodiment* – RELATIONAL PATH: <u>Grounding</u> – Goko personal and communal engagement; <u>Emergence</u> – calabash of group knowledge sharing; <u>Navigation</u> – GENE rhythm of social innovation; <u>Effect</u> – integral realities/societal transformation. RENEWAL PATH: <u>Grounding</u> – integral state; <u>Emergence</u> – institutional integration; <u>Navigation</u> – releasing GENE-ius; <u>Effect</u> – societal renaissance. REASONED REALIZATION PATH: <u>Grounding</u> – *school education for all the senses*; <u>Emergence</u> – enterprise learning and development; <u>Navigation</u> – sustainable development university; <u>Effecting</u> – institutional genealogy. • *Integrator Role*: e.g., Principal *Ivana Leskovar*, and core faculty *Karin Lavin, Mojca Pešak, Stanka Stegn*. • *GENE of Otona Župančiča Slovenska Bistrica*: grounded in *nature and children's being* – influence on community from seed to seed, building self-sufficiency; *emergence* through *constant becoming-evolution via increasing awareness*, of self and heritage, sensitive to the present and connecting to the future; *navigating* through *learning and value-based creation of knowledge and wisdom*, incorporating didactic games, publications, e-staffroom; *leveraging effective impact* through CSRE centre, engaged with communities, galvanized by European Social Fund.

For its children it supplied as much local food as possible. The kindergarten was the first to invite local producers to sew and plant for its needs. Today, each playground has a garden or a vegetable bed for which the children are responsible themselves. Thereby, they develop a responsible attitude to seeds and nature. *Children gather seeds, plant vegetables, monitor their growth, pick the fruits, gather recipes and prepare different dishes, while learning how to take care for themselves and who can help them with that.* In order, moreover, to raise awareness on healthy food, the kindergarten offered all its employees and parents education, workshops and visits to ecological gardens. The knowledge and experience, which mentors gained with the help of Slovenia's Institute for Sustainable Development, the school's eco-gardens and the eco-civil initiative of nearby Ekoci, was transferred directly into their work with children and onto their colleagues. In the final analysis, engagement with nature and ecological awareness in a kindergarten was linked to efforts with regards to individual and community development.

That brings us on to the "eastern" part of the integral kindergarten model, that is, from "southern" being to now "becoming".

Renewed becoming: constant evolution via increasing awareness

Lifelong learning and sustainable development

The staff of kindergarten Otona Župančiča Slovenska Bistrica are aware of the importance of holistic kindergarten management. This calls for interdependence and collaboration of all stakeholders who are present in the kindergarten. Therefore it is important that all of them are included in lifelong learning. The kindergarten's work can only be successful if it knows what it is striving for. *It promotes the development of every individual on a professional and personal level. It is aware of the need for personal integrity and the fact that development in one field has a decisive impact on other ones.*

The kindergarten chooses its staff with a lot of consideration and wants to participate in their education. Students already come to it in their first year of high school, when they are 14 or 15 years old. Our relationship with them, over time, is crucial, as each of them could become a future co-worker. Employees then continue the process of lifelong learning and are offered support for their professional and personal development. The development of individuals not only improves the work in the kindergarten, but also has a positive effect on the life of their family in their community. *Communication improves, knowledge on ecological topics can be applied in everyday life, the quality of leisure time improves and the independence from consumerism strengthens, thereby contributing to the sustainable development in and of the wider community.*

Awakening all the senses

In what the kindergarten terms "*sensitization courses*", run by Karin Lavin (2011) – another of the co-authors of this chapter – *teachers are introduced to new methods of work, which include ways and means of feeling, of researching and of creating. They learn how to expand their perception, how to train their attention to enhance their research capacity and their empathy, and how to deeply experience the environment and our heritage.* The exercises and results are then published and presented annually at European heritage days. The sensitization course in fact does not offer methods that you merely memorize and replicate. Instead it represents a program of personal transformation and growth. During the learning process, kindergarten teachers first discover a holographic view on the world, the environment, their capabilities and their professional role. They learn how to recognize and use the implicit knowledge that is hidden in the heritage. By being aware of their potentials and the potentials of the environment, the kindergarten teacher can offer children a more profound and holistic approach. When we feel the environment, as such, it is easier to establish a relationship based on collaboration.

S = solidarity, I = innovation, O = responsibility, K = creativity

Moreover, Bistrica, in 2013, was part of a project to increase social and cultural capital in local communities, thereby developing equal opportunities and promoting social inclusion. Slovenska Bistrica kindergarten participated in the project together with the high school SŠ Slovenska Bistrica and two primary schools. The name of the project was SI OK (are you ok): s = solidarity, i = innovation, o = responsibility, k = creativity. These were also the leading principles during the project. The three schools designed the action plan themselves, according to what they believed was missing in the city and what they could offer it. During that time, they intensely and productively cooperated with the local community and with one other.

The main aim of the project was to catalytically connect people and local communities, set within the wider ecology and society. The content of the project took into consideration the needs of various stakeholders. What was found was that there was a lack of activities in the local town that would include families (support them or socialize with them). It was felt that there was not enough connection among the locals. Since the project also included the secondary school, a lot of the goals also focused on the youth. All institutions in the town were included, societies, volunteers, individuals, etc. In a project that lasted more than a year, a lot of people were connected in various ways. The project also set the grounds for further cooperation. Activities were organized for immigrants on a regular basis coupled with cooperation with the elderly and with children with special needs. The main idea was to connect the entire local community.

The mayor of the municipality Slovenska Bistrica supported the project morally and financially. Each employee, moreover, represented an important link in the realization of the overall vision. *That brings us onto the values that form the kindergarten and to the value-based learning and value-based processes in which it engages to continuously evolve as a social system.* This then takes us to the "northern" dimension of the integral kindergarten model, our "knowing", and our sense of social responsibility.

Reasoned knowledge and wisdom: research and value creation

Ethics and values in education, in the sciences and arts

Institute for Ethics and Values: That sense of social responsibility also led Slovenska Bistrica to the project originated by the Institute for Ethics and Values of the Slovenian Academy of Sciences and Arts. After receiving an invitation for cooperation from the institute, the kindergarten reviewed its program on Ethics and Values in Education and recognized the principles, values and actions that were considered important and according to which the kindergarten works. *"The institute's intention was to expand and deepen awareness on the role of ethics, values and bioethics in forming a common future in all important areas of social activities, especially in education"* (Inštitut za etiko in vrednote [Institute for Ethics and Values], 2013). The staff (educational and technical) are aware of the fact that they have a great influence on children and consequently also on the children's parents and the broader community.

Module on Knowledge and Wisdom: In the scope of the Ethics and Values project, Bistrica first implemented the module on *Knowledge and Wisdom*, which is guided by truth, responsibility, mental openness, love for learning and knowledge, soundness, moderation and perspective. The guidelines were provided by the institute, yet the kindergarten highlighted responsibility – responsibility to oneself, fellow humans and society. In the kindergarten there is no constant control, only trust – trust that the assignments will be done responsibly.

And if you are aware that you are responsible for your actions, you will do your job responsibly and will not look for excuses elsewhere. *This module also enabled us to dive deep into "local knowledge". The kindergarten looked for people who carry wisdom inside of themselves and could teach teachers, children and their parents many valuable things.* One of the important conclusions was that everyone can contribute to society. In this way children learned about their value and the value of their parents.

A self-evaluation program

Leadership in Education: Two years ago at the time of writing, the kindergarten, in 2013, started a new activity, the self-evaluation program in cooperation with the National School for *Leadership in Education*. The kindergarten started setting new goals in a way that included every employee. All employees contributed to this process and all set out to achieve the goals. *The employees thereby received confirmation that their voices were important and that they were able to actually participate in the kindergarten's development.* Educational workers were divided into ten groups. Their leaders met regularly to discuss topics, chosen at group meetings, and they prepared common suggestions, about which the leaders later informed their groups. Educational professionals were therefore more connected and felt more responsible towards the kindergarten.

Concern for Others: The next module in the Institute's project was "*Concern for Others*" and *focused on the values of mutual respect, family happiness, gender equality, generational harmony, partnership, solidarity, and care for children, elders and people with special needs.* Concern for Others basically covered the work of the kindergarten. All the above-mentioned values were already present at the kindergarten, which accepted children and their families unconditionally. By accepting someone you show great respect for that person. The kindergarten took the needs of children and their parents very seriously. The same applied to the needs of its employees. The kindergarten constantly cooperated with parents, elders and people with special needs, which has been its practice for many years.

Life, Nature, Health: The final module, "*Life, Nature, Health*", focused on the following values: respect for life, respect for nature and the environment, health, bioethical values. This module strengthened the kindergarten's activities in the field of sensitization. It learned that its actions in this field are already very deep. The relationship to nature, life and health was already on a high level. During this module, adults learned a lot from children, who reminded all of us of everything that we often forget or do not take time to enjoy. Nature through the eyes of a child has a greater value than through the eyes of most adults.

Children still know how to feel nature. Therefore, our kindergarten is returning back to nature with the help of sensitization and is making sure that children keep this connection between humanity and nature. The upcoming modules in the Ethics and Values Project will be: Culture; Work; Creativity; Tradition; Universalism; Fairness; Integrity and Humanity. Although the kindergarten already respects all of these values, it is happy to accept the Institute's invitation, as the work will help Bistrica find a deeper meaning in its activities. Such continuous improvements in the kindergarten's learning and knowledge creation journey – that can be seen, if you like, as a social innovation – help it to increase its impact on local communities on an ongoing basis. Furthermore, its active engagement in the Citizens' Initiative for an Integral Green Slovenia inspired Bistrica to set up an Integral Care Centre, designed to leverage its impact in our communities. This brings us ultimately to the pragmatic "western" part of the integral model – also the culmination of John Heron's four modes of knowing (see Chapter 4) to "doing".

Realizing impact: the Integral CARE Centre

Reaching maturity while keeping young

The kindergarten Otona Župančiča, Slovenska Bistrica will be turning 70 in 2018. If this was a period in human life, it could be said that the kindergarten had already reached its mature age. However, it stays vital with the influx of new generations of children, parents and employees. *A kindergarten changes like a human being: it becomes wiser and more and more present in the surrounding environment. Luckily, the local communities and municipalities also make it younger by building new kindergartens.*

Our CARE Centre: integral education cannot start early enough

Generations of children get to know each other through the kindergarten and parents are given the opportunity of networking, which the kindergarten fondly supports. Each family has something to offer to others, but the school is also all vulnerable and even the strongest family can face an obstacle. Networking often helps people overcome various situations with which they are confronted. The kindergarten works on five protective factors: *resilience of parents; supporting social networks; knowledge about parenthood and child development; actual support in times of crisis; and child's healthy social and emotional development.*

In constant pursuit of opportunities for cooperation with the environment and related responsibilities, the kindergarten moreover, duly prompted through its relationship with the Integral Green Slovenia Citizens' Initiative, has decided to establish a centre that will work for the greater and common good. They call it, as embodied in our CARE quartet, a CARE centre, and in Figure 9.2 below we show its integral functioning. The aim is to intertwine the work of public services, associations and volunteers, with the intention of working for the common good. This will require constant researching of who needs what and developing plans on how to connect theory to practice to achieve our goals. The municipality of Slovenska Bistrica currently provides a space where we shall start

Figure 9.2 Kindergarten's integral care model

by offering support to families (families expecting a child; mothers on maternity leave; immigrants; and socially disadvantaged families).

Illustrating the potential for transformative education and innovation

With the help of the CARE centre, the kindergarten sees not only its engagement in the local communities becoming stronger; it is also aware of the pioneering role it can play within the Integral Green Slovenia movement, by illustrating the potential for transformative education and innovation that can be actualized by a kindergarten. Indeed, education for an integral society cannot start early enough! Interestingly, as we have seen (see volume 2,

Awakening Integral Consciousness), the same kind of CARE-ing approach is being undertaken by a higher educational institute, BC Naklo, now at a secondary and tertiary level of education. And Slovenia is a small enough country to ensure that Slovenska Bistrica and BC Naklo are in close touch, so as to join hands on their transformation journey, with due support from the Citizens' Initiative for an Integral Green Slovenia, as well as vice versa.

In the final analysis then, and overall as such, Otona Župančiča Slovenska Bistrica, in the context of an Integral Green Slovenia, is *grounded in nature and children's being – exerting an influence on community from seed to seed, building self-sufficiency; individually and communally emerges through constant evolution via increasing awareness of self and heritage, sensitive to the present and connecting to the future; navigating institutionally through learning and value-based creation of knowledge and wisdom, incorporating didactic games, publications, e-staffroom; ultimately leveraging effective impact through CARE centre, actively engaged with communities, galvanized by European Social Fund.*

We now turn from such primary grounding of integral development, in a kindergarten in Slovenia, to a recently emerging program and process of organizational learning and development in Jordan, thereby straddling the educational continuum from childhood to adulthood, and the sectoral divide between public (Slovenska) and private (MedLabs).

References

Inštitut za etiko in vrednote (Institute for Ethics and Values) (2013) Evropsko ogrodje etike in vrednot (European Framework of Ethics and Values). At http://www.iev.si/ogrodje-etike-in-vrednot/ (accessed April 2015).

Kocijančič, D. (ed.) (2002) *Naš vrtec – zdrav vrtec. Vrtec Otona Župančiča Slovenska Bistrica.*

Lavin, K. (ed.) (2011) *Kaj se kuha pod Pohorjem / What is Cooking Below Pohorje.* Unpublished.

Lessem, R. and Schieffer, A. (2010) *Integral Economics: Releasing the Economic Genius of your Society.* Abingdon: Routledge.

Piciga, D., Schieffer, A. and Lessem, R. (2016) *Integral Green Slovenia.* Abingdon: Routledge.

Soros, G. (2000) *Open Society.* New York: Little, Brown.

10 Emerging

Organizational learning and development

Summary of chapter:

1 grounding pioneering development in customer as king, group practice, quality and the pursuit of sustainability, thereby treating people well;
2 differentiated development emerged through systematization and self-organization, thereby as an effective organization;
3 currently navigating integral development via community building, conscious evolution, knowledge creation, sustainable development, building a healthy society;
4 ultimately effect moral revitalization, as self, organization, society.

Introduction: grounding individual, enterprise and societal renewal

Developing self and society

We now turn from grounding integral embodiment, in individual-and-community in a pre-school in Slovenia in the middle of Europe, on the path of reasoned realization, to an emerging program and process of organizational learning and development, in Jordan in the Middle East.

As such, organizationally in this chapter, we draw on an extraordinary group of medical laboratories, based primarily in Jordan, but also operating in the Sudan, in Irbil in Kurdestan, in Palestine and in Kuwait. The unfolding story of MedLabs, with which we, Trans4m, are also engaged in a project involving ultimately *revitalizing MedLabs' moral core*, is told here by co-founder Manar Al Nimer, who is also engaged in our Trans4m PhD program. As we shall see, moreover, both her CEO Dr Hassib Sahyoun and herself have been strongly influenced by Dutch organizational psychologist Bernard Lievegoed's approach as set out in *The Developing Organization* (2001). At the same time, MedLabs is engaged with us in becoming an

Integral Enterprise (Lessem and Schieffer, 2009). Manar Al Nimer then takes the story of herself and of MedLabs on, individually, organizationally and societally, in her own words: *beyond a one-man show.*

> Every moment from our birth till we die we are exposed to new challenges. *At every moment we learn new things, we see new people, we talk to new people, we are exposed to new cultures and beliefs, we face problems, we suffer from diseases, we graduate, we get married, we give birth, we lose loved ones and we have to deal with all of these experiences one way or another.* These are the challenges we face during our life journey. *Jordan meanwhile, that small country which has been my home throughout my adult life, with its limited resources, no oil and scarcity of water has the ambition, determination and will to stand side by side with the developed nations, albeit in its own authentic way.*
>
> It has one of the highest percentages of qualified manpower who enjoy pioneering and innovative capabilities. Time has shown that the strength of Jordan is in its people and their ability to overcome one regional crisis after the other and yet produce several successful organizations on the world stage, like our MedLabs Group, despite the difficulties we face locally and regionally. (MedLabs Consultancy, 2016)

Developing organization in society

According to Lievegoed, every organization evolves in different phases of pioneering, differentiation and integration like a human evolves from a child to a mature adult. Each organizational phase is thereby linked to a specific organizational form, leadership style and interaction with the environment. Lievegoed's Austrian colleague Friedrich Glasl added a fourth phase, the associative phase, which is closely linked to the concept of the "lean enterprise" (Glasl and Lievegoed, 2014). Further, Glasl notes that the fourth associate phase is not the end of organizational development, but there could be also a fifth phase that is beyond time and space.

MedLabs pioneered Group Practice in Laboratory Medicine in the region in 1993 through the amalgamation of four of the leading laboratories in Jordan. It transformed individual to collective behaviour and together overcame the challenges of change. These challenges were on a personal level, a governmental regulatory level, and scientific as well as financial levels. These challenges were overcome through dynamic long-term strategies set by the company's Board of Directors and implemented by its highly specialized personnel, who are dedicated to a Group Practice and to Quality of Services.

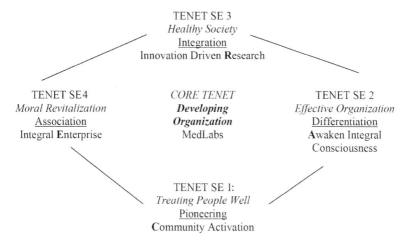

Figure 10.1 Embody MedLabs' reasoned learning and development

MedLabs' journey through the pioneering and differentiation phases, in Lievegoed's terms as we shall see, has led the organization – purposefully now towards integration – to seek to become an "Integral Enterprise", in Lessem and Schieffer's terms, thereby also becoming a CARE-ing one, for them as for us (2014), encompassing our staff and the community at large. Manar tells the MedLabs story in her own words (MedLabs Consultancy, 2016).

MedLabs: an unfolding enterprise story, by Manar Al Nimer

Individual pioneering with a group difference: planting the seeds

I feel privileged while at times still daunted to have experienced and played a part in the founding, development and now transformation of one of the largest and most respected pathology service companies in the Middle East – MedLabs. In 1987 I started as a medical technologist in one of the laboratories that eventually became one of the cornerstones of MedLabs' founding in 1993. Although this first laboratory became one of the most successful ones in Jordan between 1987 and 1993, its long-term growth and sustainability were limited by the "one-man show" business culture in the region. *From 1993 onwards a new business culture in Laboratory Medicine was created in Jordan through the formation of MedLabs Consultancy Group and I was privileged to be part of it.* This was the culture of "Group Practice". Although at the time group practice in Laboratory Medicine was commonplace in the Western world, it did not exist in Jordan or in most, if not all, the Arab countries. At the time, and I must say even to date, what MedLabs was pursuing was considered to be partly bold and innovative and partly stupid and reckless, that is, for a group of specialists to get together to create a Group Practice in Laboratory Medicine.

In 1993, then, five laboratory specialists with different sub-specialties, each with his (all the pioneers were male) own successful private laboratory, decided to combine their efforts and unite their destiny by forming the first Laboratory Medicine Company in Jordan. They gave it the name MedLabs Consultancy Group. It was also my destiny, as the one and only female pioneer (a feminine version of such), to be engaged in this bold venture from its onset.

A Palestinian refugee challenging the "one-man show"

The creation of MedLabs was built on the vision and belief of its founders then. However, this group, pioneering feat needed an individual catalyst to actually make it happen. This pioneer-and-catalyst was Dr Hassib Sahyoun, one of the founders of MedLabs in 1993. I first met Dr Sahyoun in 1986, when I worked in the Histopathology Department of a laboratory he had established with three other Laboratory Medicine Specialists in 1981. That was when he had first come back to his home Arab region, that is, now to Jordan, after spending 15 years in the United Kingdom. In the UK he had gained his PhD in Laboratory Medicine and he had worked in several hospital laboratories, thereafter gaining a postdoctoral position at the university from which he graduated, ending up with more than twenty international publications.

The laboratory Dr Sahyoun co-established in 1981 was his first attempt to develop a Group Practice in Jordan and the Region, but *this initial attempt failed due to the deep entrenchment of the regional culture in the idea and practice of a "one-man show". Therefore his individualistic partners could not recast themselves in the mould of a Group Practice.* Nevertheless Dr Sahyoun continued to lend his expertise to this original project while waiting for a second opportunity to achieve his vision. Many years later he expressed to me the frustration he had experienced during this first failed attempt, but he also told me that it had only strengthened his determination to challenge the one-man show culture in the region. I often wondered what the source of his determination and hard work was. Now, after 29 years of working with Dr Sahyoun full time under his leadership and becoming close to his whole family, *I realize that, like myself, it all emanated from his growing up as a Palestinian refugee.*

Growing up as a refugee many times over

Dr Sahyoun was born in Haifa in 1947 before the Neqbeh. During the troubles in Palestine in 1948, his father took the whole family (wife and five children) to safety to Cairo to stay a few weeks with their grandmother on his mother's side until the troubles stopped. Once the state of Israel was created, they were not allowed to return to Haifa. They then lost their home, lands, businesses, and worst of all their ties with their family and friends.

Dr Sahyoun's father worked very hard and creatively over the following ten years in Egypt to create a successful "one-man show" business in the textiles industry. However, the family had no nationality or travel documents until 1962, when a Lebanese nationality became available to them. So they then moved to Beirut, where Dr Sahyoun's father had to start all over again. In 1967, Hassib left Beirut to complete his medical laboratory studies in the UK. In 1974 the civil war in Lebanon destroyed his father's business. So once more he had to move back to Cairo for safety. The hard work and determination of his late father, combined with the insecurities generated and limitations resulting from a "one-man show" enterprise, reinforced by our insecure surroundings, had a major effect on Hassib.

Establishing the first group practice in the region: MedLabs

Hassib became convinced, through his observations and experience in life, that true success comes, on the one hand, through determination, hard work and creativity. However, on the other hand, the success of such a venture, as he directly observed, does not have long-term sustainability without converting it into an institution built on Group Practice. His father could have had the vision and insight to bring new blood into the family business, to enrich the organization and to give it long-term sustainability, but he failed to do so. Yet, to give his father credit, such a concept was even more far-fetched in the 1940s and 1950s than it is today.

This became even more apparent to the now *Dr* Hassib after experiencing the fruits of successful Group Practices and institutionalization in the UK hospitals and private institutions in which he worked after his doctoral and postdoctoral studies. This made him even more determined to follow, prospectively, the path of Group Practice. He wanted to serve and live among his Arab people, yet he wanted to build a practice that is sustainable over the long term and that could be as professional and competitive as any institution worldwide. These experiences and characteristics made him the right person to catalyse the formation of the first Group Practice in Laboratory Medicine in the region – MedLabs Group.

MedLabs, then, started with such a vision. Its core, pioneering values, as such, were to best serve their patients through Group Practice, Quality of Service, Integrity, and Leadership. While these were indeed pioneering values, at the same time within them were the seeds of differentiation (quality of service) and integration (integrity). However, they did not, at such a pioneering time, include the human element of the *spirit* or the *morale* of the organizational community at large. For MedLabs was then in its pioneering phase. The number of staff in MedLabs in 1993 was just 30 including the founders, and the number of laboratories under its umbrella was just six (today we are closer to 50 labs). During that phase, moreover, my own career was transformed from that of a medical technologist, a knowledge practitioner so to speak, with experience in all related, technical fields, to a managerial position.

MedLabs as a developing organization

Pioneering organization: ripe to "over-ripe"

For Lievegoed (2001), specifically then, and in retrospect for us at MedLabs:

> *In its pure form, a pioneer enterprise is an enterprise that is still being run by its founder. It comes into being as a result of a creative act by a human being.*

The characteristics of so-called pioneer enterprises are autocratic leadership (the Group Practice at MedLabs somewhat counteracted this), direct communication, person-oriented management, an improvisational working style, the work force or community considered to be "one big family", and the pioneer's market or environment comprised of known customers, clients or employees. And at MedLabs, as we shall see, this was to change significantly over time, as pioneering was followed by differentiation, historically, and integration, today, with of course the crises ensuing in between one and the other.

These pioneering characteristics are equally familiar to the startup phases of almost any organization focusing on any aspect of communal and societal development. Lievegoed illustrates vividly, moreover, what may happen when a pioneer organization becomes "over-ripe" and has reached the threshold of a new development. Such a stage is reached when the original strength of the pioneer organization, its closeness, has become its weakness. Often, at this moment, the founding pioneer and his/her leadership and management style are increasingly questioned by the staff and demands are made to, (a) respond in a different way to external challenges (new technologies, altered economic situation etc.) and (b) organize the operations in a more systematic, differentiated way.

Table 10.1 The MedLabs organization development gene

Embodying Integral Development: Grounding Renewal *MedLabs as a developing organization* Pioneering to integration

- *Attributes of embodiment* – RELATIONAL PATH: <u>Grounding</u> – Goko personal and communal engagement; <u>Emergence</u> – calabash of group knowledge sharing; <u>Navigation</u> – GENE rhythm of social innovation; <u>Effect</u> – integral realities/societal transformation. RENEWAL PATH: <u>Grounding</u> – integral state; <u>Emergence</u> – institutional integration; <u>Navigation</u> – releasing GENE-ius; <u>Effect</u> – societal renaissance. REASONED REALIZATION PATH: <u>Grounding</u> – school education for all the senses; <u>Emergence</u> – *enterprise learning and development*; <u>Navigation</u> – sustainable development university; <u>Effecting</u> – institutional genealogy.
- *Integrator role*: embodied leader, e.g. **Hassib Sahyoun, Manar Al Nimer**.
- *GENE of developing organization*: *Grounded* in customer as king, group practice, quality and the pursuit of sustainability, thereby **treating people well**; *emerging* through marketing and communications, HRM, science/R&D/quality/IT, thereby as an **effective organization**; *navigating* through community building, conscious evolution, knowledge creation and sustainable development, thereby building a **healthy society**; ultimately effecting **moral revitalisation**.

From pioneering to organizational differentiation and societal integration

<u>Overcoming internal imbalances:</u> MedLabs' pioneering phase lasted from 1993 till 1999. During this phase the number of staff increased to over a hundred. Spirits were still high, but things were getting chaotic due to the lack of systemization. *It was realized, then, that to continue on this journey towards a Group Practice, successfully, the company had to be organized and systemized through the transformation of its management style towards a more decentralized, self-organizing approach.* All that was learned and improvised in the first six years of the collective experience had to be documented and systemized so it could become the norm for all newcomers and new projects. Moreover, there were other, external hurdles to be overcome.

<u>Overcoming external imbalances:</u> In fact, when the decision to create a group practice in the Medical Laboratory field in Jordan had been taken in 1993, little did the founders realize the barriers they would face in the form of the Ministry of Health regulations related to the establishing and owning of a Medical Laboratory. As one would expect, these regulations were

based on and encouraged the "one-man show" culture that was historically dominant. So, *the challenges were not only to remove the internal tendency to individualize management and ownership as mentioned earlier but also to adjust to the external challenges that had been set in stone* for many years. The regulations stipulated that a Medical Laboratory should be owned by one specialist licensed by the Ministry of Health based on certain criteria. There was nothing in the regulations that allowed for a group of specialists or an institution to own a Medical Laboratory. This regulatory imbalance threatened the very existence of "MedLabs" as a group practice that was a partnership, not a "one-man show", as a limited liability company registered at the Ministry of Trade and Industry. In my capacity I was given the responsibility of getting the regulatory bodies to change their historical beliefs, laws and practices.

Overcoming my own self-doubts: I was still then in the early phase of my career, with limited experience and knowledge in laws, regulations and how they are made, and more importantly how they could be changed. However, like the founders I was a great believer in group practice. I wanted to prove to myself and to them that I could take on this challenge. Most importantly, I knew how to invite people to listen to my arguments by creating friendly professional relations with them. After two and a half years of visits, meetings, discussions and waiting patiently, I succeeded in *getting the government officials to change the regulations at the Ministry of Health to allow institutions to own and manage a laboratory, or indeed several laboratories. This was for me a cross-roads in my career path.*

The advent of scientific management: bereft of examples, we had to be creative

The number of laboratories by 1998 had increased from four to nine and the number of patients using our services had more than doubled. These were excellent results; however, they did not result in any increases in company profit. In-depth analysis of the reasons behind these poor financial results revealed that some of the systems that were originally designed and implemented were based on a centralized structure. The company's management steered many of the laboratories operations, which included centralized material management, centralized marketing and centralized staff management. This resulted in several imbalances; management became a bottleneck and was blamed by laboratory directors for any shortcomings. Laboratory directors became de-motivated and were not part of the decision-making process. In turn these directors were not accountable for their own operations, which led to spiralling expenses that in turn stunted any growth in profits.

Less centralized systems, as I have already indicated, had to be designed to remove the management bottleneck, make directors accountable for their own operations, include laboratory directors in the day-to-day decision making, make them cost conscious and most of all reward them for their success. Unfortunately there were no existing models in Jordan or in the region for such a decentralized, self-organizing group practice, from which we could draw. We had to be creative.

All Laboratory Directors' salaries were replaced by a profit-sharing system whereby they receive a percentage of the operational profit not to be less than a minimum monthly amount related to their qualifications and experience. We also decentralized materials management whereby directors became responsible for the ordering of their own supplies from MedLabs accredited suppliers. This model is still successfully applied 16 years later and continues to provide excellent results for all stakeholders. Several years after the introduction of this decentralized model, through, a new imbalance started to creep in. This was related to the staff in the laboratories rather than the directors. Although the directors were motivated, their staff were not, especially those who had been with MedLabs from early on.

This phase in MedLabs coincided with my project-based MSc program in Transformation Management, which I undertook fully supported by top management. This educational undertaking, for me, was quickly followed by the development of an annual series of lectures to all staff given by the heads of scientific departments, as well as by HR Managers for "soft" skills and QA Managers for "quality and safety". This paved the way for MedLabs to achieve its first international certification in laboratory management, the ISO Certification for Management of Medical Laboratory Services (BS EN IS0 9001:2000). Decentralization of many of the laboratory operations combined with our staff evaluation system and the overall process of creating a self-organizing culture seemed to have eliminated, at the time, most if not all of the imbalances experienced in the early days of MedLabs.

The integration phase: re-balancing the social and the technical

MedLabs' would-be role making peace between Israel and Palestine: The integration phase, of organization and society, was in fact initiated at the beginning of the MedLabs journey in 1994, when the peace plan between the Palestinians and Israel seemingly had became a reality. For several of the founding members of MedLabs and myself, *supporting the young state of Palestine was a burning issue that demanded our attention.* Early in 1995 a renowned international auditing firm was contracted by MedLabs to prepare a study of the private health sector in the West Bank and Gaza. The result of the study demonstrated that the medical private sector in Palestine was totally lacking in quality services. There was a dire need for a bold major investment to create a privately owned chain of diagnostic centres that would include laboratory and radiology services as well as an IVF centre, none of which was available at the time in the whole of Palestine.

The challenges we faced were enormous. We had to deal with both the Israeli and Palestinian regulations, importing equipment, furniture and many other items that were under the control of Israel, and each item had to have clearance. Movement between the cities required special passes from the Israeli authorities and they were not always forthcoming. In mid-1996 a hospital in Bethlehem built by an American NGO was offered for sale. This was the only purpose-built hospital in Palestine and was fully operational. The partners in the Palestinian company decided to bid for the hospital and by the end of 1996 the investors paid the NGO the full amount for it and we took the hospital over. Little did we know at the time that this would be the beginning of the end of the Palestinian joint venture. For reasons not comprehensible to me or to the partners, the Palestinian Authority blocked the registration of the hospital. All efforts made between 1997 and 1999 to try to operate it failed.

The projects that were implemented, however, included the diagnostic centres in Ramallah, Nablus and Hebron, and the IVF centre. These were divided between the partners, MedLabs ending up with the IVF centre only. This was a major blow to us after we had done all the hard work for four years only to lose a substantial part of our capital. To save the day, top management in MedLabs accepted a reduction in their earnings by a good 50 per cent, which in turn put major personal pressures on them. Thankfully by 2001 MedLabs was back on its feet financially and the crisis of 1997 to 1999 became history. Lessons were learned. Our steadfastness in the face of crisis pulled together partners and staff as at no other time. The knowledge we gained from implementing these projects was also of great value to all.

Success has its price: By 2012 in fact, 19 years after its establishment, MedLabs had became a mature enterprise, so to speak, having worked through its pioneering phase between 1993 and 1998, and thereafter its differentiated and scientific phase between 1999 and 2011. All of this enriched and cemented the MedLabs culture, making it the fastest-growing Group Practice in Laboratory Medicine in the Middle East. Furthermore, *the successful institutionalizing of Laboratory Medicine within MedLabs has provided employees with long-term job security and career paths, and led to a process of self-organization through decentralization. However, success, growth and systemization have a price!*

Over the last four years, and especially after the euphoria of achieving the highest certifications, accreditations and awards, it has become apparent that MedLabs has lost part of its spirit as a caring company. As a result, the moral core of MedLabs has been in decline. In 2012 we needed to redirect our attention to our employees and the community to reflect MedLabs in its true image as a CARE-ing Enterprise. Through identifying our inner and outer callings, we needed to be able to strongly relate to, and care for, our interrelatedness, internally and externally. *We needed to "look deep" underneath the surface, to see the generative, life-giving grounds of MedLabs. In transforming our organization from a machine to a living system, we needed now to manage by "Design".* What, then, does this need to involve, individually and communally?

Enhancing personal wellbeing: Individually and first, we continued to support the wellbeing of our clients or patients through the highest-quality standards to ensure accuracy of medical testing, information on our products and service, while at the same time *promoting a healthy lifestyle in which we make a meaningful difference in the lives of our beneficiaries.*

Moreover, and most especially at this phase of MedLabs' journey, we must understand that the life journey, for our people, has both an outer purpose and an also inner purpose. The outer purpose is to arrive at the goal or destination, to accomplish what has been set out to do, to achieve this or that, which, of course, implies the future.

However, *if one's destination, or the steps taken in the future, take up so much of one's attention that they become more important to oneself than the step taken now, then one completely misses the journey's inner purpose,* which has nothing to do with where the person is going or what he/she is doing, but everything to do with how. When you become conscious of being, what is really happening is that being becomes conscious of itself. When being becomes conscious of itself – that is presence. *The one thing that truly matters is then missing from your life: awareness of your deeper self – your invisible and indestructible reality.*

Building stronger communities: Second, creating shared communal value, for Jordanians and all other countries and markets in which we operate, *enabled us to address local issues based on the needs and expectations of our communities and partners with governmental and nongovernmental partners/stakeholders who share our values and objectives.* In 2013 and on the occasion of MedLabs' 20th anniversary, for example, all 33 branches (at the time) were opened for one day only to offer three medical tests free of charge to the general public. The initiative was carried out under the patronage of the Ministry of Health and on that day MedLabs tested over 9,000 individuals for diabetes, vitamin B12 and thyroid function. The results that were statistically significant were shared with the Ministry of Health. Together with Save the Children, moreover, MedLabs committed to testing 40,000 women and young children for iron deficiency anemia as part of a CSR project run by the Save the Children Foundation to protect women and children in refugee camps and poverty pockets across Jordan from malnutrition and illness.

Recognizing a diversity of cultures: Third, MedLabs needs to recognize the diversity of cultures in which it operates, ranging from Jordan and Palestine, to the Gulf countries, to Kurdestan and Sudan. MedLabs' first regional experience was in *Palestine*, where the population has very close ties with Jordan. There are a lot of intermarriages between Jordanians and Palestinians. There are also many Palestinians who live in Jordan as a result of the Neqbeh of 1948 and the 1967 war who still have close relatives in the West Bank. It was very satisfying for me that MedLabs started its journey regionally from my country of birth, which I relate to and feel attached to (MedLabs Consultancy, 2016). The Palestinian experience, though erratic, is successfully providing job opportunities for at least twenty-five professionals, providing a much-needed high standard of services without any losses to the mother company. MedLabs' strategy in the West Bank is long term, while providing support to the people of Palestine.

Northern Iraq–Kurdestan: The Kurdish aspirations – today we have four laboratories in Kurdestan – reminded me of my own people in Palestine. *The desire to be independent with self-rule and the suffering resulting from oppression is all very familiar. Yet they were different, which made me even more interested to study this culture that is Arab and not Arab, close and yet far.* Again the building of trust was extremely important. Overcoming the language barriers especially with the younger generation was critical, and understanding their deep culture while trying to find common ground between that culture and that of MedLabs was a significant personal challenge for me. *The challenge continues, the knowledge building continues, the give and take continues, the dialogue continues, the adaptation continues, and all of that is without having to compromise our MedLabs values,* ethics and standards enhanced by the enthusiasm of our willingness to achieve success.

Conclusion: pioneering, differentiation and integration

Overall then, and in conclusion, MedLabs, in the course of its development through pioneering, differentiation and integration, *has grounded its*

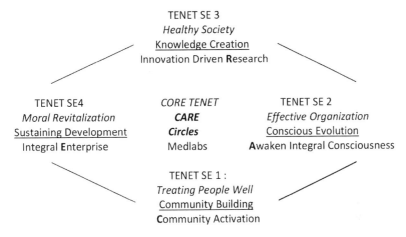

Figure 10.2 CARE circles and integral enterprise

pioneering development successively in customer as king, group practice, quality and the pursuit of sustainability, thereby treating people well; differentiated development has emerged through marketing and communications, HRM, science/R&D/quality/IT, thereby as an effective organization; integral development is currently being navigated through community building, conscious evolution, knowledge creation and sustainable development, thereby building a healthy society, ultimately effecting moral revitalization.

We now turn from emergent enterprise to *genealogical* navigation via community, sanctuary, academy and laboratory.

References

Glasl, F. and Lievegoed, B. (2004) *Change Management*, 3rd revised edn. Bern: Haupt Verlag.

Lessem, R. and Schieffer, A. (2009) *Transformation Management: Toward the Integral Enterprise*. Abingdon: Routledge.

Lievegoed, B. (2001) *The Developing Organization*. Chichester: Wiley-Blackwell.

MedLabs Consultancy (2016) The Medlabs Pulse. Corporate publication.

Schieffer, A. and Lessem, R. (2014) *Integral Development: Realising the Transformative Potential of Individuals, Organizations and Societies*. Abingdon: Routledge.

11 Effecting
Embodying inter-institutional genealogy

Summary of chapter:

1 grounded community wise, naturally/communally, in *rapoko* and *unhu* here;
2 emerging sanctuary wise, culturally and spiritually, through *ngoma lungundi*;
3 navigating academy wise through "Mode 2" Da Vinci Institute;
4 effecting laboratory wise – another world is possible.

Introduction: institutionalize development

Functional and structural genealogical sources

This penultimate chapter on inter-institutionally embodying integral development, now via the transformative effect of "north-western", *reasoned realization*, also builds on the prior "southern" *relational* and "eastern" *renewal* paths. As such we reintroduce you to the inter-institutional genealogy that you first came across in our previous volume, *Innovation Driven Institutional Research*, now by way of a practical example, in rural Zimbabwe. Moreover, this chapter builds on the prior chapters concerning <u>school education for the individual senses</u>, second on <u>organizational</u> learning, third and penultimately taking an altogether integral, <u>genealogy</u>-laden inter-institutional step, before we turn to ultimately embodying <u>integral enterprise, economic and societal development</u>.

Such an inter-institutional "genealogy", as we term it, both builds, functionally, on the seminal work of French post-modern philosopher, Michel Foucault, as generally indicated below, and also structurally on our own internal "GENE-alogy". The latter then builds on our *integral rhythm* – local *Grounding* (origination), local–global *Emergence* (foundation), newly global *Navigation* (emancipation) and global–local *Effect* (transformation) – that underlies all our Trans4mative work.

For both Nietzsche and Foucault, according to external Guatemalan-born, genealogical interpreter C.G. Prado (now Emeritus Professor in the Department of Philosophy at Queen's University in Ontario, Canada), *rather than uniformity, what is found at the historical beginning of things is disparity*, for us between "north" and "south", "east" and "west" (Prado, 2000). Thereby, in our recent book *Integral Dynamics: Cultural Dynamics, Political Economy and the Future of the University* (Lessem *et al.*, 2013), we maintained, additionally, that the release of GENE-ius requires us to interweave, and thereby co-evolve, one with the other, with the marginalized communal "south", gaining pride with at least a starting place.

Contemporary laboratory to institutional genealogy

In fact, for American cultural historians McNeely and Wolverton (2008), to whom we were first introduced in our previous volume, *Innovation Driven Institutional Research*, today's epochal historical events, most recently climate change and economic crises, have determined that *the laboratory, not the university, will continue to exercise a strong influence on learning and knowledge creation, especially in the natural sciences.* Above all, the ascendancy of the laboratory is reshaping the basic missions of other institutions, like indeed universities, pushing some towards obsolescence while giving others a new lease of life.

We beg to differ. For us, then, always firmly with our feet on the local ground, through we may reach for the global skies, so to speak, our starting point is invariably a local *community* as "southern" natural and communal grounding. Our next port of call, with our focus primarily in the "global south", where religion/spirituality is such an all-pervasive local–global phenomenon, after community, comes what we have termed

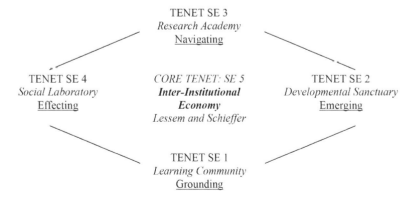

Figure 11.1 Embodiment, reasoned realization and genealogy

a *sanctuary* (monastery, temple, mosque, synagogue, retreat or even a museum or natural sanctuary) as, for us, "eastern" spiritual and cultural emergence. It is only thereafter that a disciplinary-based pre-school, school and university *academy*, philosophically and scientifically, as "northern" navigation and indeed *laboratory*, technologically and economically, as "western" effect comes into integral play.

Taking on, then, from where McNeely and Wolverton leave off, for them duly aligned with different forms of communication, we see each particular community (oral), sanctuary (scriptural), Academy (print) and laboratory (digital) as having its prospectively genealogical institutional place (see Figure 11.1 above). Moreover, it is no accident that, as American "westerners", McNeely and Wolverton award the laboratory pride of contemporary place. They have in fact argued, overall, that *knowledge has been fundamentally reinvented a number of times throughout human history*. In each case they describe how one new institution – the "library" for example (for us in particular today the "community"), the "monastery" to take another historic example (our sanctuary), then the university, and most recently the laboratory – has replaced the knowledge-based institution that preceded it. For instance, new academic disciplines served to renovate and completely redesign the old-style universities, recognizing their continuities with the ancient *universitas* in name only.

Indeed *some academic philosophers*, like the German philosopher Fichte in the late nineteenth century, *advocated abandoning the term university, so thoroughly did the new "research university" depart from the past.* Sadly, from our transformative perspective, this did not happen. So we are now, in the new millennium, taking on from where Fichte left off two centuries ago, coming up with our *institutional genealogy as a composite community, sanctuary, academy, laboratory*, both in theory and – as we shall see below – in practice. We start where we began this work, in the country of my birth, Zimbabwe, where a particular community has given rise, with us, to an embryonic genealogy.

Start CSAL with nature and community

- Drawing upon communal values
- The healing power of nature
- Revisiting Socratic method

Local grounding in human-ness: unhu here

Morgan Tsvangirai (2011), Zimbabwe's ex-Prime Minister and now leader of the official opposition, writes that reform for him,

Table 11.1 Genealogical institute

Embodying Integral Development: Navigating Reasoned Realization   *Zimbabwean Genealogical Institute*   Chinyika community to agricultural extension offices

- *Attributes of embodiment* – RELATIONAL PATH: <u>Grounding</u> – Goko personal and communal engagement; <u>Emergence</u> – calabash of group knowledge sharing; <u>Navigation</u> – GENE rhythm of social innovation; <u>Effect</u> – integral realities/societal transformation. RENEWAL PATH: <u>Grounding</u> – integral state; <u>Emergence</u> – institutional integration; <u>Navigation</u> – releasing GENE-ius; <u>Effect</u> – societal renaissance. REASONED REALIZATION PATH: <u>Grounding</u> – school education for all the senses; <u>Emergence</u> – enterprise learning and development; <u>Navigation</u> – Mode 2 University; <u>Effecting</u> – mutual support networks.
- *Integrator role*: e.g., **Muchineripi and Kada, Lessem and Schieffer**.
- *Genealogical institute*: *Grounded* **community** *wise, naturally and communally, in* **rapoko and unhu here**; *emerging* **sanctuary** *wise, culturally and spiritually, through* **ngoma lungundi**; *navigating* **university** *wise through* **Da Vinci Institute/Trans4m**; *effecting* **laboratory** *wise through the* **agricultural extension officers**.

> *will bring losses to tradition and patriarchy; losses to perceptions of political royalty; losses from our inheritance; fears of the unknown, and losses from patronage and advantage.*

For Tsvangirai as such,

> *We must manage these losses, save our institutional memory and history, and preserve our core values and those cultural aspects which define us.*

Such core values, on the one hand, for Zimbabwean Human Resource practitioner and graduate of our PhD program Dr Steve Kada, from a local Shona and Baremba (an African–Jewish sect) and a global Judeo-Christian, moral perspective, encompass *uri munhu here*, that is, "human-ness" (Lessem *et al.*, 2012).

Nature reserve: Muchineripi Rock – rapoko/Karanga

On the other hand, for the Karanga people of Chinyika, for another of our PhD graduates, son of the local chief Dr Chidara Muchineripi, from a natural, indigenous perspective, *as the Karanga are people of the soil*, he maintains that their life depends on the soil, for they till it. They grow their crops on it and draw water from the ground. They bury their dead in the soil. Soil is their power. For one elder poet, as such,

Why have the people forgotten what used to happen on Muchineripi rock?
Where your forefathers gathered rapoko and millet in abundance?
Where children played around while fathers and mothers pounded rapoko ears with sticks and winnowed the grain from the chaff?
Where granaries were filled with golden brown rapoko grains?
Arise the children of Chinyika.
Arise and be who you should be!

When people arise, from the ground as it were, in Chinyika, as they did when they saved themselves from starvation midway through the first decade of the new millennium, it was the traditional *rapoko* crop to which they returned. Drawing, as such, on nature and on community, the village elders, on the one hand, and the village's leading women, on the other, assembled on the symbolically all-important *Muchineripi Rock*, near where their former chief was buried. The initial conversations that they held, in a small hut on the top of the rock, were what initiated the whole process of renewal. It was this communal process, accompanied by rituals as old as the hills, that was to become, if you like, Chinyika's "Socratic Method".

Such face-to-face more-than-human conversations in the round, engaging with one another and with nature, resulting structurally in the formation of a strongly constituted Chinyika Community Council, formed the primal backdrop then, and the natural and communal grounding now, for an overarching genealogy, in this initial genealogical case *activating community* through creating a governing community circle. We then turn from community to sanctuary, from the local grounding, and local–global emergence, of our institutional genealogy.

Local-global museum as sanctuary

Ngoma Lungundu: locally/globally emerging through culture/ spirituality – Baremba journey

- Raising consciousness
- Religious renaissance
- Spiritual enlightenment

Sanctuary, in that emergent respect, was represented here, as we shall see, by "the lost arc of the covenant". Hitherto, orally to begin with rather than drawing on their learned literacy, the people of Chinyika (see our opening volume, *Community Activation*) challenged the exogenous status quo, whereby maize had become the externally imposed staple crop, and introduced their newly indigenous rapoko. Through, in effect, a process of informative and transformative *cooperative inquiry* (Heron, 1994) of iterative action and learning, drawing on experience and imagination, conceptualization and application, they proceeded to renew themselves, economically if not also culturally.

The overall symbolism of the *journey* thereafter, moreover, embodied in the Baremba (black Jews) and the story of "the lost arc of the covenant" – *Ngoma Lungundu* – in that emergent respect, which found its way from ancient Yemen to Zimbabwe (Parfitt, 2009), overtook that of the soil, embodied in the Karanga and in rapoko. In relation to Chinyika, the Ngoma Lungundu, besides being an artefact, has a spiritual power of renewal for the Baremba if not also Karanga communities in Gutu. This is an opportunity for the local community to look outside and connect with a global platform. While the Ngoma Lungundu "drum" (arc of the covenant) lies in peace and serenity in the museum – our sanctuary – in Harare, it is calling out loudly for the Baremba and the world, via Kada (Lessem *et al.*, 2012), to be reawakened to the values of personhood and to the integration of indigenous and exogenous knowledge.

Genealogy's sacred cause: becoming Zimbabwe

The Ngoma Lungundu provided, if you like, Chinyika and its neighbouring rural communities with a challenge to revisit their history, religion and intellectual values for the purpose of creating an integrated local and global community. Institutionally, as such, this becomes the sanctuary before and after which a university and laboratory lodge themselves, locally and globally. From a Christian perspective, the ark of the convent with its inscribed commandments is lodged in the hearts of humankind, including here in Zimbabwe. The first inscription is summarized by Christ: "*Hear, O Israel, Jehovah our God is one Jehovah, and you must love Jehovah your God with your whole heart and with your whole soul and with your whole mind and with your whole strength.*" The second is this: "*You must love your neighbour as yourself. There is no other commandment greater than this.*"

This is, for Kada, what all individuals, organizations and nations should be concerned with, acknowledging the universal sovereignty of the Creator and the practical humaneness and value sharing of southern African "ubuntu" (I am because you are). *Africa, from its heart, then, was privileged with the quality of brotherhood and human passion that it must share with the rest of the world: Steve Kada describes this as a mother's plea – 'Uri munhu here?*

This, in Zimbabwe at least, is our institutional genealogy's sacred cause. To that extent, the Harare museum, with its Zimbabwean arts and artefacts, symbols and ceremonies, should be integrally as well as dynamically interlinked with the rural soil–nature–community, such as that at Chinyika. Such a museum, as a house of culture, should contain not only the past and the present, but also imaginatively the projected future – as was the case for shona sculpture – naturally and communally, culturally and spiritually, if not also scientifically and technologically, thereby *awakening integral consciousness*, as a past–present sanctuary (Raftopoulos and Mlambo, 2009).

Towards a research academy

Globally navigating via science and philosophy

- Learning centre (*universitas*)
- Agricultural extension community
- "Mode 2" university

From nature reserve, and community, to museum-as-sanctuary so to speak, we turn, in our Zimbabwean and indeed overall Trans4m genealogical case, now to a "Mode 2" university that builds on what has come before. To that extent our partner Da Vinci Institute, with its focus on innovation, is ideally placed, together with Trans4m, to become such. In the words of an originator of the Mode 2 university, ex-President of the European Research Council Helga Nowotny:

> *Instead of being clearly demarcated from other forms of social prac-*
> *tice, and far from being uniform or unified, science itself now consists*
> *of a set of complex practices, deeply embroiled, integrated and impli-*
> *cated with society. Mode-2 knowledge production teams, as such,*
> *and collaborative organizational forms, have not only multiplied but*
> *spawned endless variants.*

Indeed, and given its position, lodged in Southern Africa, and revisiting university history, as per McNeely and Wolverton, the extension of that natural, Chinyika meeting place, *Muchineripi Rock*, into a "learning centre", would be the obvious first stage of a subsequent "*universitas*". For the *earliest universities*, in the twelfth and thirteenth centuries in Bologna and Paris, were not deliberately founded; they simply (see above) *coalesced spontane- ously around networks of students and teachers, as nodes at the thickest in these networks.*

The nature and scope of the "Mode 2" academy

In fact, it was on Muchineripi Rock that indigenous agriculturalists and exogenous extension officers first met, not to mention the spread of ICT-based connections thereafter. A newly global university such as the Da Vinci Institute, in conjunction with Trans4m, then, picks up, in Nowotny's "Mode-2 guise" in an explicit and disciplinary sense, from where nature and community, culture and spirituality, science and technology, economics and enterprise implicitly arise, in local community, and through a local–global sanctuary. The foundational, or grounding disciplines, as such, would neither be physics nor economics, nor even technology or innovation, but rather ecology and anthropology (see Chancellor William's *Constituting Africa* in our *Innovation Driven Institutionalized Research*), thereby spanning all "age-sets", in Williams' terms, and pre-school, school and university in ours.

Like the first German research universities, it would be the humanities and the "soft" social sciences, rather than, say, economics and political science, that provide the under-labouring, as it were. For whereas the universalizing sciences tend to be generalist, the humanities and anthropology are particular, to each and every person and society, be it Zimbabwe or Nigeria, Muchineripi (Chinyika) or Adodo (Paxherbals/Pax Africana). We now finally turn to the laboratory.

Genealogical laboratory

Global–local effecting via technology and enterprise: laboratory

- Agricultural/industrial labs
- Social lab/counterculture
- ICT/internet/World Wide Web

The laboratory finally, for McNeely and Wolverton, is the most evolved form of knowledge-based, or indeed knowledge creating, institution, whereas for us at Trans4m, in genealogical terms, it is the Community (Nature Reserve), Sanctuary (Future Museum), Academy ("Mode 2") and Laboratory (Knowledge Creating Enterprise), altogether genealogically constituted, in a particular society, that marks the next evolution of pre-school, school and university.

The point of departure in our Zimbabwean case, for the laboratory, within or alongside a community, sanctuary and university, is conventional (natural) science, either agriculturally or industrially (now including information and communications technology) based. In Chinyika agriculture, for example, via both so-called agricultural extension officers and mobile communications, took pride of place in that respect. As we evolve from agricultural and industrial towards social laboratories, such entities become enriched, and that is the direction in which we are moving.

Another world is possible: reinventing social emancipation

For example, the kinds of "social" laboratories, according to McNeely and Wolverton (2008), that John Dewey and Kurt Lewin established in America in the first half of the last century, are very few and far between. Yet it is that very "social" form of laboratory, which enables a "learning centre" on Muchineripi Rock, for example in Zimbabwe, or at Paxherbals in Nigeria, to become part of an institutional genealogy. Indeed, and in that very guise, the "counterculture" of yesteryear, prevalent in Europe and America, is matched today by the World Social Forum (WSF) in Porto Alegre in Brazil, as counter to the World Economic Forum (WEF) in Davos in Switzerland. One of the key academic voices in the WSF is Bonaventura De Souza Santos (2007) and for him *another world is possible*, by *reinventing social emancipation*:

- production alternatives are not only economic – their emancipatory potential and their possibilities for success depend to a great extent on the *integration of economic transformation processes and cultural, social and political* ones;
- *collaboration and mutual support networks* of cooperatives, unions, NGOs, state agencies, social movement organizations *are key* to their success;
- production alternatives and new forms of cross-border labour mobilization should *seek synergy-based relationships* with alternatives in other spheres of the economy, locally, nationally and internationally.

In the above light, that another world, or mode of production, is possible, I received a mail from Noah Gwariro, the Managing Director of Zimbabwe Power, who is a participant on our doctoral program, in response to comments I made on an early thesis submission, whereby he commented on the fact that he, though a mechanical engineer, had been passionate in his youth about biology generally, and herbal medicines specifically:

> *In fact I am so very interested in renewable-solar and bio-digesters. Bio-digesters conserve forests by using cattle manure for example to generate clean burning gas in the huts. The technology for solar and bio-digesters is developing in the Philippines after modifying basic designs from China and India. I am sure once we localize these*

versions a Chinyika version would evolve. I am elated about appropriate technology. The solar projects would allow people to consistently have light to enable schoolchildren to study in their homes. The parents would charge their cell phones at home and be able to watch television and listen to the radio. We can arrange with Econet for example to make sure there is data transmission capability around Chinyika so that the whole ICT cycle benefits these pioneers of self-sufficiency by giving them internet access. On the biology and herbal side we could have botanical gardens to preserve and propagate herbs for local use.

This would serve to constitute a social as well as a technological laboratory. We are now ready to conclude.

Conclusion: nature reserve, museum, university, laboratory

Embodying integral development in a genealogical institute

We started out with our book *Integral Dynamics*, written in 2013, when we introduced our notion of an institutional *genealogy* in this way: we quoted Senegal's contemporary sociologist Emmanuel N'Donne, reinventing the present, in his particular terms:

> *One becomes rich by taking advantage of the many canals that irrigate and diversify knowledge and wisdom, and stimulate mutual discoveries and recognition. People themselves are the main means for making this synergy work: hence the importance of supporting dynamic processes that rehabilitate people in all their dimensions, and that also rehabilitate relationships between themselves and their surroundings.*

Now, in this chapter of *Embodying Integral Development*, we returned to Africa, as it were, for *the end is where we start from*, in the famous words of T.S. Eliot.

Table 11.2 Prospective genealogical institute in Zimbabwe

GROUNDING	EMERGENCE	NAVIGATION	EFFECTING	INTEGRATING
Muchineripi Rock	Ngoma Lungundi	Learning Centre	Agricultural Extension Office	*Another World is Possible*
Nature/ Community	*Culture/ Sanctuary*	*Social Science University*	*Economic Laboratory*	*Institutional Genealogy*

And Africa is where (wo)mankind began its journey. In revisiting and indeed reinventing the journey of knowledge, at this culminating point, duly enabled by Ian McNeely and Lisa Wolverton, we have ultimately reconstituted such journey, in our genealogical terms, thereby recasting Foucault's philosophical notion in institutional terms. The overall result is portrayed in Table 11.1 above.

Institutional genealogy in Zimbabwe and Nigeria: Pax Africana

In the final analysis, and overall then in Zimbabwe, prospectively if not altogether actually, the Genealogical Institute is *grounded community* wise, naturally/communally, in *rapoko and unhu here*, thereby creating a natural and communal circle; *emerges sanctuary* wise, culturally and spiritually, through *ngoma lungundi* actualized through an innovation ecosystem; *navigates university* wise scientifically through *Da Vinci Institute/Trans4m* serving to recognize our inter-institutional; *effects laboratory wise through the agricultural extension officers and mobile communications* ultimately achieving integral enterprise, economy and society.

In the Zimbabwe case, such an explicit institutional genealogy is not yet apparent. What has evolved, in integral terms, still has a long way to go. Indeed it remains functionally implicit but not structurally explicit. As UNISA-based academics Hoppers and Richards (2011) have painfully intimated, until there is such "Rethinking Thinking", leading to a fully fledged transformation of the university to take modernity's "Other" into account, unemployment and economic crises, drugs and crime, civil war and the ultimate exhaustion of the Earth's resources, will proceed apace. Nevertheless, genealogically, there is always hope. More recently, in fact (see previous volume, *Innovation Driven Institutional Research*), a somewhat more explicit institutional genealogy has been developed by Dr Anselm Adodo as described in his forthcoming book *Community Enterprise in Africa: Communitalism as an Alternative to Capitalism* (2017), based in Nigeria around *Pax Africana*, as per *Pax Natura, Spiritus, Scientia, Economia*:

Pax Natura: *South, identified with Africa. Key features are: Indigenous Knowledge, Community activation, Agronomy, connection with the soil, respect and oneness with nature, a communiversity of life. Orientation is to Nature and Community.*

Pax Spiritus: *East, identified mainly with Asia. Key features are: emphasis on inner peace, wholeness, Culture, inner security, spirituality, higher consciousness, intuition, feelings and emotions as part of human experience. Orientation is to holism.*

Pax Scientia: *North, identified mainly with Europe. Fully in control of advances in scientific theories and social theories. Key features are: political systems, educational and research outputs, and control of world's economic, political and social systems through colonization, capitalism, socialism, neo-liberalism, globalization. Orientation is towards Rationalism.*

Pax Economia: *West, identified mainly with America. Known for business, enterprise, entrepreneurship, individual quest for profit and competition. Key features are: practical application of technology for profit, business management and dollarization of world economy. Orientation is towards Pragmatism.*

The end is where we start from

On final reflection I myself started out in life in colonial Rhodesia, hardly aware of the fact that my own ancestors, based in Buhera (a rural part of the country) had inaugurated what was termed African Trading in the 1940s together with the Chinyika-based Muchineripis. In the same way as I got seemingly diverted by classical economic principles, at the then University of Rhodesia and Nyasaland, neo-liberal economics at the London School of Economics, and by business administration at Harvard University, so the Lessems got diverted by Concorde Clothing (named after Place de la Concorde in Paris, France).

Now Foucault's genealogy, philosophically and functionally, alongside our own GENE-alogy, integrally and structurally, has come home to roost, we hope now in institutional form (institutional genealogy), as well as being functionally integral (integral enterprise/economics). In fact, we have a group of reflective practitioners in Zimbabwe, together with their institutions, now well poised to take the genealogical story on, from implicit to explicit. Altogether then, in our Zimbabwean case, altogether *genealogically, we were grounded community* wise, naturally/communally, in *rapoko and unhu here; emerging sanctuary* wise, culturally and spiritually, through *ngoma lungundi; navigating academy* wise through the "Mode 2" *Da Vinci Institute; effecting laboratory wise through the possibilities of another world of production.*

Now, with that navigational end in mind, we turn from Africa to Europe, culminating effectively in Integral Green Slovenia economy and society.

References

Adodo, A. (2017) *Community Enterprise in Africa: Communitalism as an Alternative to Capitalism*. Abingdon: Routledge.

De Souza Santos, B. (2007) *Another Production is Possible: Reinventing Social Emancipation: Toward New Manifestos*. London: Verso.

Heron, J. (1994) *Cooperative Inquiry*. London: Sage.

Hoppers, C. and Richards, H. (2011) *Rethinking Thinking: Modernity's Other and the Transformation of the University*. Pretoria: University of South Africa Press; Abingdon: Routledge.

Lessem, R., Muchineripi, P. and Kada, S. (2012) *Integral Community: Political Economy to Social Commons*. Abingdon: Routledge.

Lessem, R., Schieffer, A., Rima, S. and Tong, J. (2013) *Integral Dynamics: Cultural Dynamics, Political Economy and the Future of the University*. Farnham: Gower.

McNeely, I. and Wolverton, L. (2008) *Reinventing Knowledge: Alexandria to the Internet*. New York. Norton.

Nowotny, H., Scott, P. and Gibbons, M. (2001) *Re-Thinking Science: Knowledge and the Public in the Age of Uncertainty*. Cambridge: Polity.

Parfitt, T. (2009) *The Lost Ark of the Covenant: The Remarkable Quest for the Legendary Ark*. New York: Harper Element.

Prado, C.G. (2000) *Starting with Foucault: An Introduction to Genealogy*, second edition. Boulder, CO: Westview Press.

Raftopoulos, B. and Mlambo, A., eds (2009) *Becoming Zimbabwe: A History from the Pre-colonial Period to the Present*. Harare: Weaver Press.

Tsvangirai, M. (2011) *At the Deep End*. Johannesburg: Penguin Books.

12 Navigating
Integral society

Summary of chapter:

1   grounded in the smell of forest, a babbling brook and soft wood – we feel Slovenia;
2   as an emergent foundation, a strong bio-energetic field capable of supporting development in Slovenia is thereby in tune with the essence of life;
3   emancipatory navigation of Integral Green Slovenia is undertaken institutionally, research and innovation wise ecologically, culturally, technologically, economically follows;
4   effecting self-sufficiency, a developmental economy, a social and a living economy.

Introduction: European Community

The democratic Carantanian legacy

We now come to the end of our CARE story, presently Embodying Integral Development in Integral Society. As we had indicated in Chapter 3 of our previous volume, *Innovation Driven Institutional Research*, our attempt to ground innovation in European soils, building functionally but not structurally on the classical European Trinity of truth, goodness and beauty, ultimately fell on stony, orthodox consultancy grounds, via a Roland Berger foundation ignoring its underlying European heritage. So the European thread was picked up again, some two decades later, now turning from Germany to Slovenia, that is, from the large-scale German economic and technological powerhouse to the small-scale Slovenian natural and cultural heartlands of Europe. As such, and as we shall see, there is an emerging intimation of a veritable European inter-institutional genealogy – community, sanctuary, academy, laboratory – duly now embodied in, and effected through, integral enterprise, economy and society.

We turn then from such genealogical grounding (School-based Education of the Senses), emergence (Enterprise-based Learning and Development) and penultimate navigation (Academy-based Inter-Institutional Genealogy) to ultimately effective embodiment via *Integral Green Slovenian Economy and Society*. As such, a Slovenian Citizens' Initiative, in conjunction with Trans4m over the last three years, has focused on bringing development about integrally and effectively. A trans-disciplinary research group, in fact, bearing upon this, has involved the initiative's main coordinator, *educationalist* and environmentalist Dr Darja Piciga; Ivana Lekova, as we have seen (Chapter 9), a prominent *head teacher*; Dr Nevenka Bogataj, a *forester* and adult educator; Andrej Kranjc, a *climate change* specialist; and Marko Pogacnik, an internationally renowned *conceptual artist*, together with ourselves, Trans4m, as integral *economists*.

Integral Green Slovenia, for them and for us, then, is indeed an extraordinary research-and-development undertaking, along the emergent way – not yet fully navigationally and institutionally there – towards an institutional genealogy, as we shall see from what follows, now on the path of reasoned realization.

For Piciga and her Slovenian colleagues, on the one hand, generally speaking, they want to set their unique country, located at the European if not the world cross-roads, in its natural and cultural context, currently and historically. On the other hand, specifically, they share the actual journey towards an Integral Green Slovenian Society and Economy, the cast of characters involved, the style of leadership, the underlying conceptual model, and the philosophies and practices that underlie it all (Piciga *et al.*, 2016).

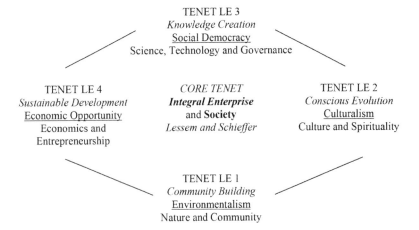

Figure 12.1 Reasoned effect of embodiment: *enterprise*/society

As you will see, these range from deeply symbolic features of the land to principles and practices adopted in the course of their transformation journey. They start then with the principality of Carantania, in the Middle Ages, which is where Slovenia's trans-cultural and trans-disciplinary journey historically started.

I communally and naturally feel Slovenia: historically and geographically

The story of an Integral Green Slovenian Economy and Society consists of a multitude of stories, of several bigger and smaller stories. First, it is historically the story about *the journey of a Slovenian community* that can be, according to historical sources, traced back, politically and culturally, to the principality of Carantania. The ancient ritual of installing Carantanian dukes in the Early Middle Ages attributed power to rulers not from God or via inheritance, but from (the representatives of) the people, during the period 664 until 1414. This democratic ceremony was, more than three centuries later, allegedly drawn upon during the creation of the US constitution. According to historical records, Carantania as an independent political entity existed between the years 664 and 745. In 1991 it was reborn, in a manner of speaking, after more than twelve centuries of subordination to various European nations and states, as the Republic of Slovenia. Moreover, it is currently a story initiated by Darja Piciga after she came across a book by Lessem and Schieffer, while visiting Geneva. That book was *Integral Research and Innovation* (2010b). But let us first continue with introducing Slovenia as a whole today.

Slovenia is small, diverse, green and beautiful. With a population of just above two million inhabitants, half living in urban areas, it covers 20,526 square kilometres and borders four EU Member States – Austria, Italy, Hungary and Croatia – with a short coastline on the Mediterranean Sea. Slovenia, geographically and ecologically, enjoys an extraordinary rich biodiversity and landscape due to its location at the junction of several ecological systems. The geographical variety of the country, covering Mediterranean, Alpine, Dinaric and Pannonian landscapes, is the basis for the high degree of biodiversity in a relatively small overall area. Variety of terrain is presented in comparatively limited plains, numerous mountainous and hilly regions, richness of surface and underground waters, and diversity of landscape as well as vast woodlands (covering approximately 62 per cent of the land). More than 50 per cent of the land is protected. Slovenia's natural endowment, moreover, has been enhanced by a tradition of close-to-natural forest management and by low-intensity farming.

It is not surprising, then, that Slovenia's brand "**I FEEL SLOVENIA**" – co-created by representatives from various areas including the civic, economic, tourist, cultural and artistic, scientific, sporting, and political spheres – emphasizes that organic development is unanimously supported by Slovenians and expresses their mission as: "Slovenia is moving forward with nature" (Piciga *et al.*, 2016). At the core of the brand is the following statement:

> In Slovenia green is more than just a colour; it is "Slovenian green", expressing the balance between the calm of nature and the tenacity of Slovenians. It speaks of unspoilt nature and the peoples' focus on maintaining it that way. . . . We never remember Slovenia only through images. A memory of Slovenia combines the smell of a forest, a babbling brook, a surprising taste of water, and the softness of wood. We feel Slovenia.

Slovenia's brand connects nature and community (humanity) in the following way:

> We wish to contribute and preserve Slovenian green for future generations.

Slovenia's crisis of values: towards resolution

However, after fewer than twenty-five years of sovereignty, and although Slovenia was initially praised for a seemingly non-problematic transition from a socialistic self-management system to the Western European concept of a market economy, since 2012 austerity measures have been imposed by the EU and international institutions in Slovenia due to a combination of economic, financial and political crises, interpreted also as a crisis of values. It is more than obvious, then, for Piciga and her colleagues (2016), that Slovenia needed to seek an alternative path out of these crises, through an innovative linking of natural and cultural traditions and present technological and economic potentials. And indeed, a number of individuals, groups, organizations and communities are striving for this.

Slovenia's comparative advantages thereby include, for example, *forestry, rich biodiversity, its geographic location, the natural environment, water availability and quality, its people, culture, heritage* – altogether as an important starting point.

Located at the European cross-roads

There seems, moreover, to be a particular strong relationship between the Slovenian natural environment and the Slovenian national character.

Challenging natural circumstances, such as mountainous landscape, harsh climate, Dinaric drought, steep Alpine slopes with many settlements close to the growth limits, have altogether been decisive for one crucial dimension of the Slovenian character: extreme overall rationality. In pursuit of the path of reasoned realization, then, *the need to use natural and human resources efficiently contributes to Slovenian innovativeness in coming up with new organizational and management forms*, such as the Commons in rural communities.

Throughout Slovenian history, then, nature and community were strongly intertwined. Already in the initial (pre-Christian period) conceptualization of Slovenian culture, a three-fold interpretation of the Earth dominated. This is today represented in the Triglav, Slovenia's highest mountain with its three peaks, being the single most revered natural feature in Slovenia. It is also featured in the national code of arms and the national flag. Slovenians, moreover, have never been invaders. While the origins of the Slovenian peoples are usually attributed to Slavic settlers, there is more to the Slovenian heritage than that, for example related to invasions of these historical lands by the Venetians (Bor *et al.*, 1989). In addition, *historical migrations by Germans, Romans and Finno-Ugric peoples caused the development of the particularly syncretic Slovenian character*, also associated with the Christian religion combined with agricultural production.

While Slovenians themselves, then, have never been invaders, they were historically exposed to a large number of cultural influences, often ending up as being subjugated, controlled or colonized. That resulted in the development of a particular strength of character, strongly attached to the homeland and with a robust sense of independence.

That exposure also resulted in a highly developed multicultural competence (e.g. speaking foreign languages) also evident from cultural variety (of dialects and folk songs). Overall, then, despite being shaped and shaken by an overall stormy past, there are clearly recognizable features of a Slovenian character tangible still today.

Given the multiple crises Slovenia is currently facing, therefore, the country has entered a process of revisiting its identity in order to find an authentic development path into the future. That is, as we shall see, where an integral economic model comes in, that overtly builds upon the moral core of a particular society, Slovenian in this case, as an inner anchor for any authentic economic development. This moral core is deeply sourced by the national character of the society and its people, including its physical nature, as well as its underlying identity, to which we now more specifically turn. We are guided by Slovenia's conceptual artist Marko Pogacnik, who has focused on Slovenian identity.

The identity of Slovenia: European sanctuary

Geography and folklore

The question of identity, for Pogacnik (2007), may have only a symbolic meaning, not connected to the practical issues of political, social or economic development. However, if the identity of a given country starts to be perceived from the standpoint of integral physical-and-human nature-and-culture, including the economy, this is more poignant. In this context, *the features of a country's identity represent the basic potentials that can be activated to enable successful and fulfilling development.* Pogacnik proposes three groups of potentials that need to be researched and developed: first *nature*, taking into account, as we have seen, Slovenia's geographical position and other characteristics of its natural environment; second cultural *symbols*; and third *folklore*.

Geographic conditions and vital connections

Primeval powers: In its core position in Europe, Pogacnik maintains, Slovenia's potential is to hold the bridge between the Balkan region and Central Europe. Compared with the human body, the Balkan region can be associated with the pelvic cavity. *Representing the belly of Europe, the Balkan is that region that concentrates and emits the primeval powers of the Earth that are capable of giving vitality and emotional upsurge to creative projects.* Central Europe, however, stands for the treasury of cultural memory and for the logical methods of thinking and planning. If these two poles are not united, either the emotional power is missing, or the capacity to proceed in a logical way is not there. Slovenia, then, is to embody the synergy between the polarities. Slovenia has the capacity to link the logic of the mind with the primary powers of life, or, in our integral terms, the path of reasoned realization and the relational and renewal paths.

Co-existence between opposites: Second, Slovenia, as we have seen, represents the only place in Europe, as intimated above, where the three large national families and language groups that constitute the European culture meet: the Romanic, Germanic and Slavic, that is, apart from the Finno-Ugric. This means that *Slovenia inherits the capacity to interconnect elements that are very different in their character and yet belong together to form a greater whole.* This quality of connecting diverse elements can function also as a means of balance between opposing forces. Such balancing between opposite positions can serve to promote peace as well as creativity.

Connecting underground regions with the surface: Slovenia, moreover, is known worldwide for its innumerable caves and extensive underground spaces distributed throughout the whole country except in its extreme east. The strong relationship with such underground spaces means that Slovenia, for Pogacnik, is a country that holds open portals of consciousness linking the underlying causal and spiritual world with the material surface. *If Slovenia has a strong connection to the realm of the archetypes, it means that it is a land open to inspiration from the universal library of Earth memory* – with great potential to support human creativity.

Slovenia holds a strong link with nature: Slovenia is one of the rare countries in Europe that has its greatest part covered by woods. *Trees*, according to Pogacnik, *represent the channels of breath running constantly between the core of the Earth and that of our home star, the Sun.* Being a place of intense exchange between the planetary powers of the Earth and the cosmic powers of the Sun means that Slovenia is not only a healthy place to live, but also *a region with a strong bio-energetic field that is capable of supporting development, being thereby in tune with the essence of life.*
    We now turn more specifically to Slovenian folklore and symbols.

Slovenian folklore and symbols

Sensitivity towards the essence of nature: One of the dominant figures in the Slovenian folk tradition, according to Pogacnik, is the figure of "Desetnica", "The Tenth Daughter". Tradition demands that if a tenth daughter is born in a family she must, once turned adult, leave the home and wander in the world all life long. "Desetnica" represents a feminine figure dedicated to the subtle worlds of nature. She can understand the language of plants and birds. If translated into logical language, this symbol means that *hidden within the psyche of Slovenian people is the capacity for great sensitivity*, which is one of the preconditions for a sustainable civilization that is in tune with nature and whose people are sensitive to each other's needs.

Love towards one's homeland: Another important feminine figure in Slovenian folklore, Pogacnik says, is "Lepa Vida", the "Beautiful Vida". The story goes that, having experienced difficult conditions at home, she accepted the invitation of a black man to be brought to the Spanish court to breastfeed the Spanish prince. While feeding the prince, she desired to go home and take care of her poor family. The folklore tradition properly mirrors one of the fundamental characteristics of Slovenian people, that is, to be loyal to their homeland and to not be afraid of challenges that they find there. Rather, *in the most dangerous moments they are capable of developing extreme creativity and dedication to the cause that inspires them.* It is a quality that, for example, came forward during the process in 1991 to 1992, when Slovenia became an independent country.

Sticking to a positive vision: Among the masculine figures in Slovenian folklore, the one of King Mathias is the most often mentioned, representing the king that is responsible for country and its inhabitants. However, he is not present now, but is "sleeping" with his "army" under a mountain. The image implies that presently we are living in a world that is unjust and often aggressive towards individuals. But within the matrix of the nation – which means, inherited within its subconscious archetype – there are sleeping potentials that are capable of waking up in certain situations, bringing into play positive visions that can help to overcome the present obstacles. *The myth of the sleeping king always ends with the promise of his awakening and reconstructing the world of justice.*

The quality of humour: Another masculine figure, for Pogacnik, from Slovenian folklore should be mentioned: "Kurent". He represents a figure of

Table 12.1 Integral society

Embodying Integral Development: Effecting Reasoned Realization Integral society Integral Green Slovenia
• *Attributes of embodiment* – RELATIONAL PATH: Grounding – Goko personal and communal engagement; Emergence – calabash of group knowledge sharing; Navigation – GENE rhythm of social innovation; Effect – integral realities/societal transformation. RENEWAL PATH – Grounding – integral state; Emergence – institutional integration; Navigation – releasing GENE-ius; Effect – societal renaissance. REASONED REALIZATION PATH: Grounding – school education for all the senses; Emergence – enterprise learning and development; Navigation – inter-institutional society; Effecting – **integral society**.
• *Integrator role*: e.g., **Darja Piciga**.
• *Integral society: grounded in **the smell of forest**, a babbling brook, and soft wood: we feel Slovenia; as an emergent foundation a strong **bio-energetic field** capable of supporting development in Slovenia is thereby in tune with the essence of life; emancipatory navigation of Integral Green Slovenia undertaken institutionally, **research and innovation** wise ecologically, culturally, technologically, economically follows; effecting **self sufficiency, a developmental economy, a social and a living economy**.*

a wise merry fellow. In his striving for freedom, he has the courage to argue with God or to climb the cosmic wine plant up to the heavens. Kurent refers to that aspect of the Slovenian potentials that can be described as *the capacity to encounter difficult situations in life with humour and clever persistency.* It is a quality that is often needed in times of crisis when human dignity is suppressed. In the final analysis, then, there can then be no sustainable and innovative development at different levels of society if the inner potentials, and consciousness, of a given country or individual are not included to support creative efforts. Activating such natural and cultural potentials of Slovenia, to a sustainable economic end, then, is in fact the vision of the Integral Green Slovenia movement. We shall now, in brief, retrace the steps of the specific Citizens' Initiative for *Integral Green Slovenia*, which is trying to bring to life the natural and cultural potential that Marko Pogacnik has depicted.

Social science and technology: an emerging research university

Towards an integral, low carbon economy

It is almost impossible to tell the story of the Integral Green Slovenia movement from a single perspective. In fact it was and is, for Piciga, a multidimensional, multilayered process to which a large number of people and institutions have contributed, and which was influenced by a rich diversity of research and development, as well as by national and international events. The initial and innovative institutional research impulse came, in fact, in the beginning of 2012 from *Professor Matjaž Mulej, a leading social scientific researcher in the fields of systems theory and social responsibility and a tireless promoter of social innovation in the Slovenian economy and society* (Piciga *et al.*, 2016). *Following his invitation*, through an IRDO – Institute for the Development of Social Responsibility – 2012 Conference, *the idea of Slovenia's development as a model of integral, low carbon economy and society was presented for the first time.*

In the period from November 2012 to March 2013, the policy planning processes in which Darja Piciga participated as a senior expert at the Ministry of Agriculture and the Environment, led her to the conclusion that in such Slovenian policies there were already important facets of the theory developed by Lessem and Schieffer (2010a) of *Integral Economics* (such as corporate social responsibility, social entrepreneurship, green economy) on which they could build, and which were a further extension of their prior work familiar to Piciga from Lessem and Schieffer's *Integral Research*. She also realized that these concepts were built on ethical cores that Slovenia and Lessem/Schieffer shared and *all served to promote self-sufficiency, a developmental economy, a social and a living economy.* A crucial milestone on the path was the foundation of the Citizens' Initiative for an Integral Green Slovenia, prepared and signed by a group of more than twenty distinguished Slovenian experts, and widely communicated in April 2013.

The Citizens' Initiative of Slovenia: integral economy and society

The "Integral Green Slovenia Citizens' Initiative for a Wholesome Life in the Internationally Respected Community of Slovenia" (Piciga, 2013) began with the following address:

> *Dear Citizens of the Republic of Slovenia,*

> *We turn to you, convinced that Slovenia has realistic possibilities of becoming within a decade a respected eco-country, a mutually cohesive and inclusive society with a thriving economy and a high quality of life, space and the natural environment. Beyond that, we also have a tremendous opportunity to become the first country to systematically implement an integral model, i.e., model of the wholesome, collaborative and integrative.*

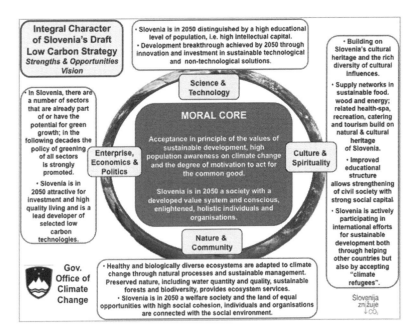

Figure 12.2 Integral Green Slovenia

The establishment of Slovenia as a globally recognised example of an integral sustainable society and economy would constitute a solution to the current social, economic, financial, political and moral crisis in our country and would assist other countries to more successfully addressing global challenges.

To believe in the prospects and feasibility of such a vision of development, we have at the disposal solid arguments; also, we can show a number of potentials and already viable examples of good practices, both globally and domestically. This vision is already built-in in the strategic plans for the 2014–2020 period. We stand before such a developmental path because we know that it is consistent with the values, attitudes and needs of the vast majority of the population of Slovenia. Under the condition that we all prove our credibility, we can together gain a lot of international support, including financial, for Integral Green Slovenia. Such an approach should also help to avoid the impending "Greek scenario". Therefore, we invite you to:

- *Firstly, gain knowledge about different economic models and sustainable development paths, to get success stories and opportunities for implementation;*
- *Secondly, support the development strategy for Integral Green Slovenia and request from those who have the decision-making power or aspire to get it, to incorporate and implement it – in their local community, in their region, in the country;*
- *Thirdly, contribute with your own work and efforts to its implementation – in a collaborative, integrative way, by incorporating positive examples, as well as by searching international support for it.*

Based on this initiative, Piciga had the opportunity to organize, with the help of her colleague Andrej Kranjc and other supporters, the first visit of Ronnie Lessem from Trans4m in Slovenia in May 2013. This eventually culminated in 2016 with the publication of our book, *Integral Green Slovenian Society and Economy: IGSE*. The Integral Green Slovenia movement, moreover, was oriented towards policy and decision makers in the EU, concerned with environmental, economic and social policy, including those in the European Parliament and other policy and decision makers on an EU level.

Conclusion: towards an integral economic laboratory

Given that the Slovenian Citizens' Initiative for an Integral Green Economy and Society only started for real in 2013, after the initial IRDO impulse in 2012, much has been achieved in less than three years. Here we have provided a short overview of its story, embodying integral development, societally to date. Over that period, the Initiative managed to grow into a highly diverse group of individuals, institutions, initiatives and enterprises across all societal sectors, and across a wide variety of social science, life science and humanities disciplines – with each one contributing a vital piece to the Integral Green Slovenian mosaic. Overall, *the case has been made, in integral theory and practice, for an alternative to economic austerity, building on Slovenian nature and culture, that is simultaneously oriented to social and technological innovation, sustainable development and the creation of new sources of livelihood.* Slovenia, a small country located at the heart of Europe, is thereby introduced as a pilot case of an integral society and economy: *grounded in the smell of forest, a babbling broo, and soft wood – we feel Slovenia; as an emergent foundation, a strong bio-energetic field capable of supporting development in Slovenia is thereby in tune with the essence of life; emancipatory navigation of Integral Green Slovenia undertaken institutionally, research and innovation wise ecologically, culturally, technologically, economically follows; effecting self-sufficiency, a developmental economy, a social and a living economy.*

What has not yet been achieved, though, is to lodge this Citizens' Initiative, explicitly, as an institutionalized research project and process within one academic or research institute, in particular, further to its initial promotion through IRDO. Instead, for the time being, it is spread across a wide range of such political, economic, ecological and cultural, and institutionalized research entities, with Darja Piciga thereby promoter of a research laboratory, so to speak, on self-sufficiency, as well as a developmental, social and living economy, together with close Slovenian colleagues and with Trans4m.

To look at what has been achieved another way, though, while many a *community* is involved in the Citizens' Initiative (see our previous volume, *Community Activation*, Chapter 8) and artist extraordinaire Marko Pocagnik is a kind of "one-man cultural *sanctuary*", not to mention also the public, private and civic *laboratories* involved, as such enterprises, the closest we have to a research *university* engaged with the initiative is Biotechnika Naklo, though the remarkable Slovenian kindergarten Otona Župančiča Slovenska Bistrica (see Chapter 9, this volume) has an active research group that has established a social innovation centre of its own. We finally turn to our Epilogue, whereby we accredit CARE now as a whole.

References

Bor, M., Šavli, J. and Tomažič, I. (1989) *Veneti naši davni predniki*. Ljubljana: Editiones Veneti.

Lessem, R. and Schieffer, A. (2010a) *Integral Economics: Releasing the Economic Genius of Your Society*. Abingdon: Routledge.

Lessem, R. and Schieffer, A. (2010b) *Integral Research and Innovation*. Abingdon: Routledge.

Piciga, D. (2013) Integral – wholesome, collaborational and inclusive – path towards green economy. In: Hrast, A. *et al.*, eds, *8th IRDO International Conference Social Responsibility and Current Challenges 2013*, Maribor, Slovenia. Maribor: IRDO. At http://www.irdo.si/skupni-cd/cdji/cd-irdo-2013/referati/e-piciga.pdf (accessed: August 2015).

Piciga, D., Schieffer, A. and Lessem, R. (2016) *Integral Green Slovenia*. Abingdon: Routledge.

Pogacnik, M. (2007) *Sacred Geography*. Great Barrington, MA: Lindisfarne Books.

Epilogue
CARE-ful self-assessment

The alternative route maps set out below, from Community activation to Awakening integral consciousness onto *innovation driven institutionalized Research*, and now ***Embodying integral development*** as a whole, all featured here, constitute the three respective, alternative paths – "southern" *relational*, "eastern" *renewal* and "north-western" green *reasoned realization* – that enable you to assess/accredit your pursuit of CARE, most especially institutionally but also individually. What is important to bear in mind, is that such a pursuit of CARE, individually and collectively, is not simple, a linear and sequential process. Elements of Community activation will continue, GENEtically, throughout your Awakening of integral consciousness, innovation driven Research and now *Embodiment of integral development*. Rome, or overall CARE, was not built in a day, or even in a decade!

ReLational Communal activation GENE

Fulfil livelihoods (G), establish permaculture (E), participatory research (N), marketing to community building (E)

Relational communal grounding and origination: fulfilling livelihoods

1 underpinned by ubuntu ("I am because you are");
2 you add natural and communal value;
3 you build up social capital organizationally and/or communally;
4 culminating in communal/organizational common ownership.

Relational emergent communal foundation: establishing permaculture

1 you pursue Earth justice, balancing "wild" and "natural" law;
2 healing the Earth through eco-economic exchange;

3   you also <u>build cultural, social and economic worth</u> organizationally/
     societally;
4   <u>participating</u> communally/organizationally <u>in the great work of nature</u>.

Emancipatory relational navigation: participatory action research

1   you <u>recognize a community's life world</u> (*vivencia*);
2   enhancing such via <u>people's self-development</u> organizationally/
     societally;
3   reinforced via action research, in alternating <u>action and reflection
     cycles</u>;
4   you consolidate on this by continuously <u>animating the whole community</u>.

Transformative relational effect: marketing to community building

1   via socio-economic exchange you <u>provide a value base to a community</u>;
2   build on community/organizational culture <u>via justice and reconciliation</u>;
3   <u>social business</u> becomes the means of micro- or macro-navigation
     for you;
4   making a powerful effect through <u>work or community-based
     democracy</u>.

ReLational Awakening of integral consciousness GENE

*Integrative humanism (G), southern world (E), relational research
(N), people economics (E)*

Relational grounding of integral awakening: integrative humanism

1   you <u>tap into</u> the <u>cultural/spiritual sources</u> of your organization/society;
2   harness and <u>synthesize strengths to obviate weaknesses</u>;
3   you <u>adopt laws of integrativity</u> (A and B both true), <u>and complementarity</u>;
4   bring about a massive web of reality <u>via different scientific traditions</u>.

Relational awakening: emergent foundation – southern world

1   you incorporate integral <u>realities</u> – <u>diverse worldviews of people/
     communities</u>;
2   releasing integral <u>rhythms</u> – out of <u>local identity towards global integrity</u>;
3   identify integral <u>realms</u> – <u>nature, culture, technology, economy, polity</u>;
4   draw initially on integral <u>rounds</u> – <u>self, community, organization, society</u>.

Relational awakening: emancipate and navigate – relational research

1   you begin especially with <u>descriptive</u> research <u>method/origination</u>;
2   you move prospectively to <u>phenomenological</u> research <u>methodology/ foundation</u>;
3   you penultimately focus in particular on <u>feminist critique/emancipation</u>;
4   culminating over time with <u>participatory action research/transformation</u>.

Relational awakening: transformative effect – people economics

1   <u>work</u> you ultimately create <u>is a livelihood</u> for individuals providing for their needs;
2   such <u>work</u> provides a context <u>to actualize your</u>/their greatest <u>potential</u>;
3   this <u>work is a focus for cooperation</u> continually between yourselves;
4   <u>work provides</u> ultimately necessary and <u>useful goods for your people</u> and society.

ReLationally innovation driven institutionalized <u>R</u>esearch GENE

Constitute the south (G), communiversity (E), social Research Paradigm (N), social economy (E)

Relational research grounding and origination – constitute the south

1   you anthropologically <u>constitute original democracy</u>;
2   your interactive Linkages in <u>temporary federations continually reform</u>;
3   <u>you evolve male and female age sets</u> as social, economic and political systems;
4   through <u>cooperatively self-governing</u> mutual consensus.

Emergent emancipatory relational research: <u>communiversity</u>

1   <u>Pax natura</u> underlies nature and community and is thereby local;
2   <u>Pax spiritus</u> underlies culture and spirituality as a Pax Africana-based sanctuary;
3   <u>Pax scientia</u> underlies science and technology and thereby a research academy;
4   <u>Pax economica</u> underlies economy and enterprise, as a social laboratory.

Relation research emergent foundation: social research paradigm

1   you pursue a <u>quest for social innovation</u> – via a relational orientation;
2   uncovering <u>why social innovation lags</u> behind technological innovation;

3   you turn individual, <u>analytic method into</u> societally <u>transformative method</u>;
4   you collectively find a way to <u>institutionalize social research and innovation</u>.

Relational institutional research effect: social economy

1   <u>grounded in sovereignty of labour</u> and subordinate nature of capital;
2   via <u>cooperation between academy, laboratory, enterprise</u>;
3   navigating via <u>participatory management, personalism, cooperativism</u>;
4   ultimately effecting your/their <u>cooperatively based social economy</u>.

ReLational Embodiment of integral development GENE

Leadership as legacy (G), knowledge rhythms (E), social innovation (N), environmentalism to sustainability (E)

Individually grounding relational embodiment: leadership as legacy

1   bringing in <u>harmony and value</u> as grounding – *Goko Routungamiri*;
2   leader emerges as a good person/<u>sacrifices for our benefit</u> – *Kupira*;
3   enabling to know – <u>without the other, there is no knowledge</u> – *Kuzivisana*;
4   effect through the <u>spirit of accomplishment</u> – *Ane Mweya Wechakati*.

Organizational relational embodiment – knowledge rhythms

1   experiential relational mode of <u>socialized knowing</u> – Ubuntu/Unhu;
2   imaginative externalized <u>knowing through metamorphosis</u> – Hosho;
3   testing of knowledge conceptually via <u>knowledge combinations</u>;
4   practical <u>knowing, through internalization</u> – Denhe re Ruzivo.

Organizational/societal embodiment: social innovation

1   basic research – origination – rediscover your local context;
2   applied research – foundation – a unique life world/reveal its meaning;
3   navigate by giving voice to the marginalized/decolonizing minds;
4   undertake collective action, develop self/community – social innovation.

Societal relational embodiment: environmentalism to sustainability

1   Ground – community building aligned with <u>environmentalism</u>;
2   Emerge – conscious evolution functionally aligned with <u>culturalism</u>;

3   Navigate – knowledge creation aligned with <u>social democracy</u>;
4   Effect – <u>sustainable development</u> – creating a world without poverty.

ReNewing Communal activation GENE

Communiversity (G), vitality of place (E), study circles (N), social business (E)

Grounding and origination of communal renewal: <u>communiversity</u>

1   your community activation is <u>underpinned by nature power</u>;
2   <u>furthered</u> through fusing tradition and modernity, <u>prayer and work</u>;
3   consolidated upon by <u>combining nature, sprit, science, economy</u>;
4   you ultimately establish a <u>form of communitalism/communiversity</u> within/without.

Emergent foundation of communal renewal: <u>vitality of place</u>

1   underpinned by your creating an underlying <u>socio-economic value base</u>;
2   enhanced <u>by communal relationships</u>, within your enterprise and/or without;
3   societally <u>embedded in the vitality of</u> your particular <u>place</u>;
4   <u>resulting in trade and accumulation</u> both micro and macro in nature.

Emancipatory navigation of communal renewal: <u>study circles</u>

1   <u>you renew</u> genuine interest in <u>individual and collective learning</u>;
2   <u>enhanced</u> by the informal character of your <u>study circles</u>;
3   navigated via a <u>flexible framework to support learning</u> and development;
4   resulting in collective <u>learning, of/through self, community, organ-</u>ization.

Transformed effect of communal renewal: <u>social business</u>

1   you begin by creating <u>community to provide the economic value base</u>;
2   you individually and collectively <u>start the economic engine at the rear</u>;

3   building up towards <u>creating a micro-world without poverty</u>;
4   such community building results in the <u>proliferation of social business</u>.

ReNewed Awakening of integral consciousness GENE

Consciousness spectrum (G), innovation ecosystem (E), institutional ecology (N), HR to conscious evolution (E)

Ground conscious renewal: consciousness spectrum

1   newly evoking the <u>ancient Indian chakra energy spectrum</u>;
2   altogether providing an <u>antidote to the clash of cultures</u>;
3   <u>as a spectrum of consciousness</u> and integration, individually and organizationally;
4   turning <u>creative vision into total quality</u> management.

Awaken renewal: emergent foundation – innovation ecosystem

1   grounding and origination of consciousness – <u>local identity</u> – <u>stewardship</u>;
2   an emergent foundation as a <u>local–global "non-entity"</u> – <u>catalyzation</u>;
3   co-evolve <u>newly global</u> emancipatory navigational <u>entity</u> – <u>research</u>;
4   ultimate transformative effect leads onto <u>global integrity</u> – <u>facilitation</u>.

Awaken renewal: navigate emancipation – institutional ecology

1   <u>Ground</u> – <u>activate</u> community through a <u>communal learning</u> initiative;
2   <u>Emerge</u> – <u>awaken</u> cognitive, affective, behavioural, value-laden <u>awareness</u>;
3   <u>Navigate</u> – <u>research academy</u> in economic, educational, communal sectors;
4   <u>Effect</u> – <u>embodying sustainable development</u> – socio-technical laboratory.

Awaken renewal: transformative effect – conscious evolution

1   <u>grounding in spiritual consciousness</u>, not in labour as a commodity;
2   emerging though a <u>co-evolved knowledge</u>-based evolutionary spiral;
3   co-navigating <u>via a conscious organization</u> based on a full spectrum;
4   <u>effected through conscious evolution via Japanese-style kyosei/co-evolution</u>.

ReNewed Embodiment of integral development GENE

Integral state (G), institutional integration (E), release economic GENE-ius (N), societal renaissance (E)

Renewed grounding of integral embodiment: integral state

1   a grounded commonwealth – association and spirit of public belonging;
2   an emergent regime securing acceptance and legitimacy in wider society;
3   competent administration – reliable, trustworthy public institutions;
4   able leadership gives rise to an ultimately integral state effect.

Emergent renewal: towards institutional integration

1   individual evolving – <u>entrepreneur, manager, leader, integrator</u>;
2   organization evolving in stages – <u>pioneering, differentiation, integration</u>;
3   an integrated organization – <u>learning to knowledge creating enterprise</u>;
4   effect transformation – <u>commonwealth to organizational ecosystem</u>.

Navigate renewal: releasing economic GENE-ius

1   grounded in <u>local–global movement</u> aligned with community activation;
2   emerge <u>middle–up–down–across</u> via awakened integral consciousness;
3   embodied in an economic <u>research and development centre</u>;
4   commit to <u>resolve burning issues</u> embodying integral development.

Effecting renewal: bridging the gulf – societal renaissance

1   Grounded relationally in <u>diverse worlds</u>;
2   Emerging renewal wise through such, <u>blending tradition and modernity</u>;
3   Navigating reason wise though <u>community-based democracy</u>;
4   Effecting realization through <u>distributed revenues</u>.

ReNewed innovation driven institutionalized Research GENE

Commonwealth (G), social ecology (E), integral academy (N), operations to knowledge creation (E)

Grounding and origination of research renewal: commonwealth

1   your research is <u>embodied in</u> spiritualized religion via a <u>commonwealth</u>;
2   furthered through <u>a marriage between different worlds</u>;

3   natural, economic, cultural and social systems <u>lodged in spiritual science</u>;
4   whereby you <u>reclaim the land and renew enterprise</u>/community/society.

Renewed foundation of institutionalized research: social ecology

1   you <u>replace "I am because I have power"</u> with "I am because we are";
2   <u>emerging via spirit, rhythm and creativity</u> set within our GENE;
3   <u>navigating new meaning</u>, motif, ethos, mode, function, method <u>and form</u>;
4   <u>affecting a social ecology</u> – leadership, knowledge and industry ecology.

Emancipatory navigation of institutional research: integral academy

1   a <u>community academy</u> serves to institutionalize community activation;
2   a <u>developmental academy</u> serves to awaken individual/group con-
     sciousness;
3   a <u>research academy</u> underlies innovation driven, institutionalized research;
4   an <u>academy of life</u> is one where transformative education takes place.

Transformed effect of institutionalized research: knowledge creation

1   you ground origination in a <u>knowledge and value base</u>;
2   emerging <u>middle–up–down–across</u> through a <u>knowledge crew</u>;
3   you navigate via a <u>hierarchical business or academic functional system</u>;
4   you effect via a <u>networked</u>, autonomous, interdependent <u>project layer</u>.

ReaSoned realization of <u>C</u>ommunal activation GENE

Self-government (G), disclose new worlds (E), wealth of networks (N), mutual advantage (E)

Grounding/origination of communal realization: <u>self-government</u>

1   you <u>engage in direct democracy</u>;
2   evolving through the <u>evocation of a big restorative picture</u>;
3   amplified by a <u>discursive community</u>;
4   effected via individual and group <u>individuation to actualize a truth quest</u>.

Emergent foundation of reasoned realization: disclose new worlds

1   you exhibit/<u>encourage virtuous citizenship</u> in your enterprise or without;
2   enhanced by <u>cultivating solidarity</u> in your enterprise and/or community;

3   consolidated by <u>disclosing</u> altogether <u>new worlds</u> within or without;
4   altogether engaging in <u>social, cultural or economic history making</u>.

Emancipatory navigation of reason realization: wealth of networks

1   you <u>provide commons-laden purpose</u> to your community/organization;
2   <u>enhanced through peer-to-peer</u> relationships in such;
3   building socially and technologically <u>through open source connectivity</u>;
4   results in <u>community-based</u> and <u>institutionalized research networks</u>.

Transformed effect of reasoned realization: mutual advantage

1   <u>soil, river, forest</u> provide the <u>value and research base</u>;
2   you become <u>purveyors of your region as institutional researchers</u>;
3   build on such through a <u>provincial diversity of socio-economic structures</u>;
4   effect via <u>powerful cultural, political, economic local government (zemtsvo)</u>.

ReaSoned realization of <u>A</u>wakened integral consciousness GENE

Integral theory (G), spiral integral (E), integral innovation (N), integral awakening (N)

Awakening reason: grounding/origination – integral theory

1   Wilber's <u>4 Quadrants</u> – intentional, behavioural, socio-technical, cultural;
2   all Quadrants/<u>all levels</u> – egocentric, ethnocentric, world/centric;
3   <u>multiple intelligences</u> – logical, verbal, spatial, interpersonal, intrapersonal;
4   subject to <u>states and types</u> – gross, subtle, causal; and masculine/feminine.

Awakening reason: emergent foundation – spiral integral

1   alternate between individual expressive and collective sacrificial;
2   accommodating a double helix – memetic structure and prevailing conditions;
3   you emerge in two tiers – survival to egalitarian, flex/flow to holonomic;
4   your culminating effect is to promote human (self/societal) emergence.

Awakening reason: emancipatory navigation – integral innovation – TIPS

1   you focus on <u>people – managing self and others;</u>
2   you systemically manage <u>interdependence and complexity – systems;</u>
3   you promote <u>innovation – "Mode 2"</u> production of new knowledge;
4   resulting in <u>social and/or material technologies.</u>

Awakening reason: transformative effect – integral awakening

1   <u>uncover soil, soul, society</u> relating to nature, self and social relationships;
2   reveal Earth democracy to <u>understand ourselves as planetary beings;</u>
3   <u>realize knowledge society</u> for sustained and inclusive growth;
4   as Sarvodaya herald the <u>integral awakening of all – self, community, world.</u>

ReaSoned realization of <u>I</u>nnovation driven <u>R</u>esearch GENE

Truth–goodness–beauty (G), integral development (E), reinvent knowledge (N), solidary economy (E)

Grounding reasoned institutional research: truth, goodness, beauty

1   institutionalized research is <u>grounded in truth, goodness and beauty;</u>
2   emerge through <u>scientific, managerial and artistic creativity;</u>
3   navigated via <u>phases of creativity, elaboration and orientation;</u>
4   effected by <u>innovators – entrepreneurial, scientific and artistic.</u>

Emergent reasoned institutional research: integral development

1   centred in community – <u>co-creating ecosystems,</u> community activation;
2   culture – <u>renew self, organization and society,</u> awakening consciousness;
3   innovation – <u>regenerating knowledge,</u> institutionalized research;
4   impact – <u>social innovation</u> – actualizing development.

Emancipatory navigation of reasoned research: reinvent knowledge

1   conceive of an <u>integrated genealogy</u> rather than a standardized university;
2   research aligned with <u>community, sanctuary, academy, laboratory;</u>

3   connecting and renewing <u>oral, scriptural, textual and digital</u> forms;
4   interactive laboratory <u>releasing GENE-ius</u>/recognizing GENEalogy.

Transformative effect of reasoned research: solidary economy

1   institutionalized research <u>grounded in rainforest eco-services;</u>
2   via <u>"mestizo logic" – cultural democracy</u> reverses cultural imperialism;
3   development measured by <u>quality of attention given to people/culture;</u>
4   effect by <u>reimagining trade experimenting with ideas/institutions.</u>

ReaSoned Embodiment of integral development GENE

Educate individual senses (G), organizational learning and development (E), inter-institutional genealogy (N), integral economy and society (E)

<u>*Educating the senses*</u>*: Otona Župančiča Slovenska Bistrica Kindergarten*

1   grounded in nature and being – influence on community via seed to seed;
2   emergence via constant evolution and awareness, of self and heritage;
3   navigate via learning and value-based creation of knowledge and wisdom;
4   leverage effective impact via a CARE Centre for Social Innovation.

<u>*Organizational learning and development*</u>*: MedLabs Group in Jordan*

1   pioneer – grounded customer care, group practice, quality, <u>sustainability;</u>
2   differentiate – emerge through systematization and <u>self-organization;</u>
3   integrate – consciously evolve – navigate – building a <u>healthy society;</u>
4   realize as a whole – effect <u>moral revitalization</u> of self, organization, society.

<u>*Inter-organizational genealogy*</u>*: Chinyika, Da Vinci, Trans4m Globally*

1   Grounded nature and community wise – <u>learning community;</u>
2   Emerging culturally and spiritually – <u>developmental sanctuary;</u>
3   Navigating scientifically and technologically – <u>research academy;</u>
4   Effecting economically – another world is possible – <u>social laboratory.</u>

Develop integral economy/society: Integral Green Slovenia

1   Grounded in the forest smell, babbling brook, soft wood – <u>feel Slovenia</u>;
2   Emerging <u>bio-energetic field</u> capable of supporting development;
3   emancipatory Navigation – <u>ecological, cultural, technological, economic</u>;
4   Effect <u>self-sufficient</u> economy, <u>developmental, social</u> and <u>living economy</u>.

Index